tongues of fire

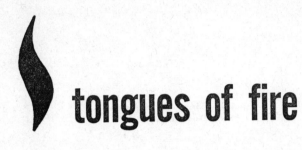

tongues of fire

Leonce de Grandmaison, S.J.

TRANSLATED BY M. ANGELINE BOUCHARD

FIDES PUBLISHERS   NOTRE DAME, INDIANA

BY THE SAME AUTHOR:

We and the Holy Spirit
Come Holy Spirit

Published originally in French under the title of
Écrits Spirituels, II, "Retraites," and *Écrits
Spirituels*, III, "Dernières Retraites et Triduums,"
pp. 1-76, by Beauchesne et Ses Fils, Paris,
France, 1934.

LIBRARY OF CONGRESS CARD CATALOG NUMBER: 61-17234

table of contents

I. THE FOUNDATIONS OF THE APOSTOLIC LIFE

1.

Fear of God 1
Repentant, Purifying Love 3

2.

Humility 6
Work 8

3.

The Religious Virtues 12
Fraternal Charity 16

II. THE PASSION OF OUR LORD

1.

The Law of Charity and of Service 21
Jesus the Ransom and the Victim of Sin 23

2.

The Passion of the Flesh 25
The Silence of Jesus 26

3.

The Passion and the Sensibilities of Jesus 27
The Passion of Honor 29

4.

The Death of Jesus 30
The Sacred Heart 31

III. OUR LIFE HIDDEN IN GOD

1.

The Death of Sin 33
Death to Sin 35

2.

The Risen Life with Christ 36
Putting on Christ 38
Mary, Guardian and Model of our Life
  Hidden with Christ in God 40

3.

Our Life Hidden with Christ in God 41
The Sweetness and Efficacy of This Life 43
Note on Devotions 44

IV. CONFORMING OUR LIFE TO THE LIFE OF CHRIST

1.

The Fundamental Truth 47
The Will of God 49
Application of the Fundamental Truths
  to the Apostolic Life 51

2.

Sin 53
The Sins of the Apostle 55

3.

Note on Lukewarmness and Spiritual Dryness 57
Reforming our Will 58
Reforming our Mind 59

4.

Note on Compunction 62
The Presentation of Jesus in the Temple 62

V. THE MEANING OF LIFE

1.

The Meaning of Our Life 65
The Use of Creatures 67
Note on Three Ways of Meditating Simply 70

2.

The Parable of the Talents 71
Compunction 72
The Inevitable Penance 75
Note on Corporeal Penance 76

3.

On the Parables of Mercy 78
The Apostolic Call 79
The Apostolic Call of Jesus 82

4.

On Three of Jesus' Words on the Cross 85
The Preferences of Jesus 87
Note on Interior Peace 89

VI. THE CALL TO THE APOSTOLIC LIFE

1.

Jesus Leaves His Mother to Enter the Apostolic Life 91
Note on Mental Prayer 92
The End of Man 94
My Disordered Passions 96
Returning Everything to God 98

2.

The Presentation in the Temple 100
The Abasements of Christ 102
Contempt for Self 104
The Consecrated Man 106

3.

The Temptations of Christ 109
Note on Penance 109
The Apostolic Vocation 111
Various Answers to the Call 113
The Annunciation 116

VII. THE LIFE OF FAITH

1.

The Sterile Fig Tree 119
The Life of Faith 120
Loving All Things in God 123
Note on Mental Prayer 125
Convincing Ourselves of Our Nothingness 127

2.

The Fall and Repentance of Peter 129
We Are Sinners 132
Advice on Spiritual Courage 134
Our Disordered Faculties 135
Advice on Sacrifice 138
The World and the Spirit of God 139

3.

The Visitation 142
Note on Penance 143
The Apostolic Call 144
Note on Discretion 145

Can You Drink My Cup? 147
Note on Abnegation 149
"I am thy servant" 150

4.

Meditations on Two Beatitudes 152
Bethlehem 154
Note on Scruples 156
The Flight Into Egypt 157
And Jesus Advanced in Wisdom 158

5.

Meditation on a Few of Our Lord's Last Words 161
Note on Election 161
The Bonds of Jesus 163
The Crucifixion 164

VIII. THE PURIFICATION OF THE APOSTLE

1.

I am the Lord 167
The Use of Creatures 170
God is Love 174

2.

The Mission of St. John the Baptist 177
Sin Outside of Us 177
Sin Within Us 180
The Fundamental Virtues — Obedience 182

3.

Fidelity to the Grace of God and Vigilance 185
The Apostolic Profession 186
The Offering to the King 190
The Fundamental Virtues — Work 192

4.

The Two Standards 195
Jesus in the Temple 198
The Fundamental Virtues — Self-Forgetfulness 200

5.

The Spirit of Jesus 203
Conforming to the Tastes of Jesus 204
The Obedience of Jesus 209
The Fundamental Virtues — Interior Mortification 211
The Compassion and the Waiting
of the Blessed Virgin Mary 213

I

THE FOUNDATIONS OF THE
APOSTOLIC LIFE

1.

Fear of God

"Unless the Lord build the house, they labor in vain who build it" (Ps. 126:1). That is why we are going to try to lay a few foundation stones. Or better still, we are going to see under what conditions we ourselves can be these stones, with God's help.

The first foundation is fear of the Lord. This is *a revealed truth*: "The fear of the Lord is the beginning of wisdom" (Prov. 1:7). Fear is the first gift of the Holy Spirit, the foundation of the delightful knowledge of God that is Wisdom.

It is also *a truth of experience*. Whenever God wants a soul to progress, whenever He chooses to entrust to a soul a mission for the good of many, He inspires it with the gift of fear. Thus Jeremiah's "Ah, ah, ah, Lord God! Behold, I cannot speak, for I am a child" (Jer. 1:6). And St. Peter's "Depart from me, for I am a sinful man, O Lord" (Luke 5:8). And St. Paul's cry as he reached out "trembling and amazed" for someone to take his hand: "Lord, what wilt thou have me do?" (Acts 9:6).

1

Mary also knew fear before the Incarnation: ". . . she was troubled at his word, and kept pondering what manner of greeting this might be" (Luke 1:29). And later: ". . . and thy own soul a sword shall pierce" (Luke 2:35).

Our Lord Himself experienced fear: "Now my soul is troubled. And what shall I say? Father, save me from this hour!" (John 12:27). ". . . and he began to feel dread and to be exceedingly troubled" (Mark 14:33).

In all these instances there is diversity of mode, but a deep underlying unity.

Finally, it is *a truth of reason*. Fear is a fundamental gift because it roots us in the truth about God and divine things. These things are terrible: the ways of God, the justice of God, the mercy of God, the silence of God, the holiness of God. They are beyond us, above us. A child has no fear amid terrifying and unknown forces. He does not realize that if he touches a live wire or climbs over a high fence it will mean death. A man knows these things and fears. And so, in the face of the supreme manifestations of God's omnipotence — hell, the Cross, heaven, the call to souls, absolution, the Eucharist — those whom the Holy Spirit places under His influence, those whom He penetrates and inspires, fear.

And they fear when they turn and look within themselves. Here again the truth is terrible. There is the sight of our sins. (Are any of us innocent of sins of egoism, vanity, self-love, sins against charity, sincerity, sins of sensuality, sins of omission?) And there is our frailty. (Without special help from God, what would we have done on a certain day, at a certain hour? What choice would we have made? Without His continuing help, what would we do tomorrow?)

When we stand before these two abysses — the abyss of the infinite purity of God, the only Good, inaccessible to the sinner, and the abyss of our own wretchedness and weakness — we are seized with an impulse to retreat, to dread. This is not a matter of distrust, nor of discouragement or despair. It is a piercing, poignant, and purifying view of what we are in very truth before the eyes of God. As long as we have not been purified by this sentiment, we cannot say that we have tasted the Lord. It is fear that first makes us know and experience what God is and what we are. It brings the Infinity of God out of the domain of concepts, words, and naked faith, into the realm of truths that are felt and perceived. Whence the importance of the gift of fear, and the fact that every authentic contact with the divine increases, broadens, deepens, and purifies this gift in us, and makes our faculties for knowing and loving receptive to God's grace.

In union with the Church, let us ask the Holy Spirit for this gift: "Pierce thou my flesh with thy fear" (Ps. 118:120). "O Lord, give us a perpetual fear as well as love of Thy holy Name."[1]

We might add that we have good reason to fear. For we are face to face with a beginning, with a new course that will lead us God knows where, but in the end "through the cross to the light" (providing it is the course God wants for us). We have reason to fear because "if anyone wishes to come after me, let him . . . take up his cross, and follow me" (Mark 8:34).

Now this fear is not servile or disturbing, but "chaste." That is to say, it is born of love and creates in us an eager and peaceful solicitude to serve better, to love better, a resolve not to turn a deaf ear to God's call, not to allow the power for good that He entrusts to us, the talents that He has given us to this end, to be lost or perverted in any way.

Repentant, Purifying Love

It has been well said that fear (understood in the sense of fearing not to love enough, fearing not to be able to love,

---

[1] Concluding prayer of the Litany of the Most Holy Name of Jesus.

fearing not to be worthy of loving, as explained earlier)
is the timid sister of tenderness. That is what makes fear
so active, so genuinely efficacious.

For this chaste fear, this fear that is the servant of
love, the envoy of love, does not depress, discourage, or
afflict the soul. Rather does it stimulate the whole soul to
purify itself, to strive to be less unworthy, to be holier.
The greater the love, the more demanding it is. To labor
at this task is to lay down within ourselves the second
foundation: the foundation of repentant and purifying love.

Repentant love separates us from evil and from the
evil things we have done, desired, craved, or perhaps pur-
sued. For we are accomplices of sin at all times in some
obscure way, by being on good terms with it through our
secret instincts and by being in contact with it through
bad example and incessant, multiform incitement. Repentant love separates us from sin by making us wage war
against it through our efforts for personal perfection and
our apostolate. Well, we must realize that sin, always so
close to us, is an evil, and the only real evil.

Sin is a great evil because it alone perverts human des-
tinies in a way that can be irreparable. The end of the
parable of the foolish virgins proves it: ". . . and the door
was shut. . . . 'Sir, sir, open the door for us!' But he answered and said, 'Amen I say to you, I do not know you' "
(Matt. 25:10-12). The door is closed, it is useless to wait
any longer.

Sin is a great evil because it renders the Precious Blood
of our Lord Jesus Christ ineffectual. Our Lord gladly
gives His blood. In His agony in the garden, He gives His
whole body, like grapes under the wine press. At this price
anyone who wants to can come and wash himself in the
purifying fountain. At the scourging, He says: Here are
my shoulders, my arms, my chest, my body. At this price,
the sensual are redeemed. At the scene of the mocking,
He gives His head. At this price He buys back the proud,

the leaders, those in responsible posts whose guilt is great. On Calvary He gives His feet, His hands, His heart. At this price, He redeems the forgetful, the negligent, those who have not searched, who have not loved, who have not willed in time.

Is not everything accomplished? No. Defeat is still possible. We still have the power to sin. Therefore, let us not love our sins. We must hate them, reject them, prevent them, wipe them out. That is repentant, purifying love. Our love and our work will always bear the mark of a debt, an expiation, a reparation. For others, of course. But first of all for ourselves. There will always be cause for penance, for conversion, for repentance, for burning tears.

You may say: We are worth more than so many others! We have been so much more faithful! No, you would not say such a thing, because it would be so childish. Say: We have been greatly protected, sought after, privileged. But that also creates obligations. *Kyrie Eleison!* Lord, wash me still more from my iniquities.

Ours is a *purifying love* because we are concerned with the sins of others. The ideas of evil, goodness, and of the greatest good that our associates, friends, and relatives have — indeed their very rule of action and behavior — will depend in large measure on our attitude toward sin. Our life work, our known profession of piety, our education will always make of us criterions for others. The more they admire us, the more they will look to us as standard-bearers. This is the meaning of the peasant's words to St. Francis of Assisi: "Take care to be as good as people say you are, for many are those who have put their trust in you."

Well now, what idea do we want to give others? What idea do we give them now? When others see us act, do they realize that the greatest evil is not to be poor, humiliated, suffering, totally lacking in joys and pleasures? In looking at us do they understand that the great evil is sin, forgetting God, jeopardizing our salvation? What is the over-all lesson our life teaches? Are others better, more sincere, closer to God, purer, more charitable, after having been exposed to our influence? Is our repentant love purifying?

The work of the apostolate demands pure souls. That is the first condition, the *sine qua non*. It is the first foundation of perfection, of love of our Divine Lord.

Suggested Reading

The Gospel According to St. Luke, 14:25-35.

The Imitation of Christ, Book III, Chapters 1, 8, and 9.

. . . and I will not give my glory to another. Hearken to me, O Jacob, and thou, Israel, whom I call. I am he, I am the first, and I am the last (Is. 48:11-12).

Who are You, my dear Lord and God, and who am I, the lowliest earthworm among Your servants! My beloved Lord, how I want to love You! My Lord and God, I give You my heart and my body — but how joyfully I would do more through love of You, if I knew how! (St. Francis of Assisi).[1]

2.

Humility

Humility is normally acquired by cordial meditation on the life of our Lord who "emptied himself" (Phil. 2:7), and also by accepting humiliation when it comes to us. Humility makes us pleasing to God and to men. It is the hidden pearl. Hence anyone who wants to lead a perfect life, an apostolic life, must make extensive use of the normal means of acquiring humility.

Each one of us will be humiliated:

Because our efforts will always be relatively futile. Even if we possessed the greatest powers of persuasion,

---

[1] As quoted by J. Jørgensen, *St. François d'Assise: sa vie et son oeuvre* (Paris, 1909), p. 106.

we would ultimately reach few souls, and even those more often than not in a superficial way. Many souls escape us, many abandon us. We shall never offer all that is needed to meet the needs of minds, hearts, and wills. They will come to us begging. We shall have nothing to give. Others will do better than we.

Because we shall never measure up to our hopes, our desires. We shall encounter great defeats and small. Life always shipwrecks a part of our dreams. Our health may collapse or be precarious. We may lack the leisure we need. We may fail in our efforts to teach others, to convert others. In our spiritual life, we may run head-on against faults that appear invincible: discouragement, dryness, interior trials, indifference, etc.

How, then, can we profit from humiliation in order to attain humility?

Our mental attitude in the face of life's humiliations should consist of a twofold judgment: 1) I am fallible: I have and shall continue to have illusions both in the direction of *presumption* and of *pusillanimity.* On the one hand, I may think I have more courage, initiative, intelligence, steadfastness, and supernatural endowment than I really have. On the other, I may think I am less capable, more fragile, and more blundering than I am. Conclusion: I must not be too quick to imagine that I am not appreciated, or that I am useless. There is often need of a person of lesser stature. Heroic good-will is always useful, and sometimes indispensable. 2) I must accept being reproved, admonished, guided. For we sometimes have glaring defects visible to everyone but ourselves. And I must be willing to help others to correct their faults.

Our heart's attitude in the face of humiliation will consist in accepting it sincerely, without bitterness, as a salutary tribulation, and in drawing the normal conclusions that will put us in our place as servants. Thus: A person like me must be available for service of all kinds. I must be willing to be called upon for anything and everything, except when it conflicts with the just, necessary, and indispensable demands of my interior life and of my health. I must be ready to be among those who are crushed with work — ready to be disturbed, to be imposed upon, to be given difficult assignments, to be used, to be expected to lend my knowledge and my small talents to others, and to be satisfied with the fate meted out to me by God, by my work, my friends, my colleagues.

Finally, what attitude of will should we take in the face of humiliation? This is an important point. Humiliation is naturally depressing in its various forms, whether it be brought about by ill-health, our own failings, or defeat. The humble will springs back under humiliation and keeps trying, thus restoring the soul's courage and confidence. "For when I am weak, then I am strong" (2 Cor. 12:10). Humiliation is the thorn in St. Paul's flesh, the messenger of Satan buffeting him. "Concerning this I thrice besought the Lord that it might leave me. . . . 'My grace is sufficient for thee'" (2 Cor. 12:8).

This, then, is our conclusion: Despite our wounded sensibilities, our failures, our dark imaginings, and real defeats, we must start all over again, persevere, do better, and correct our mistakes when we have made a bad beginning or completed a task poorly. Those who are always improvising are either angels, mediocrities, or sluggards. The initiative of the humble is always fruitful, sometimes heroic, and always holy. The basic condition is to forget ourselves, to realize that we don't matter or at best matter very little, and to keep our eyes on our Lord who took "the nature of a slave" (Phil. 2:7).

Work

In the matter of penances, let us choose those that are demanded of us — authentic, practical, commonplace penances, those that are willed by God. And first among these is work, understood in its apostolic sense.

Sometimes, almost always in fact, our work will hold

some attraction for us. An effort will be made to put the right person in the right job. Naturally speaking, we shall enjoy our work, whether it be teaching a class, or giving individual guidance to someone who is intelligent, perspicacious, well-bred. But we shall never have only the work we love. There will always be secondary tasks that are necessary but often very earthy, tiresome, monotonous. We would like to have the pleasant without the unpleasant.

Besides, once we have overcome our initial inexperience and our first discouragements, even work we love sometimes becomes tedious in the long run. The cloth is threadbare. We are bored with the beauty of Madame de Sévigné's *Letters,* with the geometry of the triangle. Even when we love our work, there are hours when it is hard, when we would like to slip away, retire, and rest. But we must go on. Then the great law of work for all men, "In the sweat of thy face shalt thou eat bread" (Gen. 3:19) weighs heavily upon us. No one completely escapes or circumvents it. As for us, we must love our work and accept it totally, wholeheartedly. When the sun shines straight down, the wheat grows riper and the flour will be whiter.

And so, making all due allowances, we dare say that a divine alchemy brings forth an eternal treasure from our really laborious work.

It may also happen that the very nature of our work is distasteful to us. True, those in charge make every effort to make the right choices, and the success of an undertaking demands that each one be placed according to his aptitudes. Even so there are positions to be filled and tasks to be done regardless of individual preferences. We are often obliged to do things we do not like, such as supervising and reprimanding others, organizing material resources, begging for funds, etc. Then our work becomes a heavy cross, although habit and courage can make it lighter. It remains acceptable, pleasing, only in one important respect: it is service. "My food is to do the will of him who sent me" (John 4:34).

Finally there are certain aspects of all apostolic work
that make it very meritorious, sanctifying, and reparative.
Apostolic work must be *disinterested*. And education in
particular is necessarily a matter of self-giving. We are
planting oaks. Education is disinterested because it always
involves a disappropriation of our affections, and sooner
or later it calls for effective detachment and separation.

The affective disappropriation consists first of all in not
demanding of those we are serving or trying to serve any
immediate human reward. "Do good . . . not hoping for
any return" (Luke 6:35). This applies not only to financial
returns, but also to little gifts on birthdays and anniver-
saries, expressions of affection, and the like. We cannot
always avoid these things, and we must even demand some
of them of the children in our care as a matter of training.
But we must not insist upon or take pleasure in them, or
manifest human displeasure if they are not forthcoming.

Moreover, we must not appropriate for ourselves any
sentiments of affection, trust, or esteem that others have
for us. Our Lord must remain the one first loved, first
served. And we must not exact from our friends and pupils
a kind of hyperdulia. Now, I am not saying that we cannot accept and benefit from holy, faithful, and tender friendships, providing they are pure. But we must not be too
possessive in this matter. A man speaks of his house, his
wife, his factory, his work, his literary creations. He is
free to use them as he sees fit. But we are not working for
ourselves. We are working for the Lord.

The time may come when we shall be called upon to
practice effective detachment from a certain occupation, a
certain place, a certain pupil, a certain possession. Our
poor habits may be firmly rooted partly through routine,
partly through natural attraction. And now we must go
somewhere else, and do something else.

Another aspect of truly apostolic work is that it is of
indefinite duration. The great dream of many men is to

retire. To this end they will sacrifice many things. They look forward to the day when they will live as they please on their own land.

Rest, retirement, time to ourselves, leisure when we want it. Our work is hard now. But we are moving toward deliverance, toward peace. And yet not so. An apostle's work is never finished. The only retirement for him is a forced retirement. He yearns to die in harness. And if he cannot work any more, he knows the inaction that God commands is a labor that has its price. He prays, he hopes, he offers up. His work does not have the earthly prospects of reward which are so sweet and appealing. His treasure is in heaven "where neither rust nor moth consumes" (Matt. 6:20). His life is hidden in God with Jesus Christ.

Suggested Reading

The Imitation of Christ, Book III, Chapters 3, 4, 8, and 10.

Follow Me. I am the way, the truth, and the life. Without the way there is no going; without the truth there is no knowing; without the life there is no living. I am the way which thou must follow; the truth which thou must believe; the life for which thou must hope (*Imitation,* Book III, Chapter 56, 1).

Thou hast taken my right hand; thou wilt guide me with thy counsel, and then thou wilt accept me in glory.

Whom have I in Heaven but thee? And if I am with thee, earth does not delight me.

My flesh and my heart faint away, the Rock of my heart and my portion, God forever (Ps. 72:24-26).

In that very hour he rejoiced in the Holy Spirit and said, "I praise thee, Father, Lord of heaven and earth, that thou didst hide these things from the wise and prudent, and didst reveal them to little ones. Yes, Father, for such was thy good pleasure" (Luke 10:21).

Come to me, all you who labor and are burdened, and I will give you rest. Take my yoke upon you, and learn from me, for I am meek and humble of heart; and you will find rest for your souls. For my yoke is easy, and my burden light (Matt. 11:28-29).

3.

The Religious Virtues

Holy Mother Church officially bases the life of striving toward perfection upon three virtues, which all religious are required to profess and to practice under vows. It is a serious matter. It would seem, therefore, that these virtues must have an important place in the lives of all who are resolved to seek perfection, hence in the lives of all apostles.

The virtue of poverty. The purpose of the vow of poverty is to destroy lust for temporal goods at its very root. Our Lord knew that "where thy treasure is, there also will thy heart be" (Matt. 6:21); and that many men see their treasure in temporal goods, in money. Such men may look upon money as the direct cause of pleasure. (Witness the self-assurance of the rich man who struts about, knowing that all doors will open to him, who is pleased with himself, who thinks everything is due him.) Or they may consider money as a means of obtaining pleasure. (All pleasures, or almost all, even the most delicate such as the praise of men, expressions of esteem, can be bought and sold.) Whence the necessity of breaking this bond to allow the soul to soar heavenward.

Thus, when the man said to Jesus: "Master, I will follow thee wherever thou goest," He answered: "The foxes have dens, and the birds of the air have nests; but the Son of Man has nowhere to lay his head" (Matt. 8:19-20). And to the rich young man, He said: "If thou wilt be perfect, go, sell what thou hast, and give to the poor [here poverty is a means] . . . and come, follow me [the way to the perfect life is opened by this sacrifice]" (Matt. 19:21). Finally, there is the First Beatitude, the foundation of the perfect life: "Blessed are you poor" (Luke 6:20). And St. Matthew adds: "in spirit" (Matt. 5:3). This is a compelling formula that explains the First Beatitude and gives us a lever, a means of entering the perfect life, even if we should retain a certain amount of property, of material goods.

Poverty of spirit consists in keeping little or nothing that is superfluous, in not holding on to, or being attached to the goods of earth. Of course the superfluous, which is a material concept, depends a great deal on situations, propriety, needs. A very rich family, living in great style, may have nothing superfluous. It is the attachment that makes the difference. This is what the First Beatitude states emphatically and explicitly. Money is a good servant, but a very bad master. Even when we are using it, we must control it, and not take a fancy to it. On the contrary, let us be detached from it, and know how to do without it gladly when necessary, in the measure that God pleases to have us do without it.

"Lady Poverty" is a friend of our Lord's. Let us not treat her as if she were a kill-joy or a streetwalker. Let us even honor her from time to time by making a small sacrifice of our comfort or self-love. In all that, we need discretion and guidance. The heart of the matter is not to cling to money, not to depend on it, and not to encourage in others the feeling that the principal thing in life is to *have,* to be rich.

The virtue of chastity. In this connection we have already said all that needs to be said with regard to the purity of souls that want to serve our Lord efficaciously. But two points need to be made:

a) The spirit and the practice of the virtue of purity are compatible with the married state. (Consider the two Saint Elizabeths, Saint Bridget, Saint Jane de Chantal, the two Marys of the Incarnation, etc.) The need here is for liberty of soul with regard to the pleasures of the senses, a liberty obtained through prayer, vigilance, and mortification.

b) Souls undergoing serious temptations can remain very pure. God sometimes permits these temptations to afflict innocent souls in order to instruct them, humble them, make them more compassionate of others, and also

to inure them to dangers (as in the case of St. Catherine
of Siena).

In an apostle's life the virtue of purity must shine forth
to the point of being contagious. Individuals may, if they
are inclined to do so, place their resolutions under the
protection of a vow. All apostles must increase and
strengthen the angelic virtue in their souls by nurturing
the efficacious causes of purity in their lives.

First of all, modesty, a vigilant watch over the senses,
over the imagination, over the mind (in the matter of
entertainments, reading, affections). We must, however,
avoid becoming scrupulous, worrying over trifles. After
seeking guidance, we must act straightforwardly against
vain anxieties, unfounded fears. But while there are things
that we must be able to look at or at least see, know, and
read, there are others that we must ignore, hold in contempt, and forget. And the rule is not the same for all.
Besides, we must practice a wise mortification, which may
vary greatly according to our state, our health, our inclinations, our tendency toward a joyful or gloomy temperament,
our age, and our occupation. In this matter, spiritual direction, discretion, as well as liberty, are indispensable.
"Let not him who eats despise him who does not eat" (Rom.
14:3).

Finally, the most efficacious cause of purity is union
with our Lord in a strong love, a love that is deep, personal,
generous, delightful. Now this cause is always available
to us. Frequent and if possible daily Holy Communion has
great efficacy for us and for the souls of others under our
care. We must love our Lord as our "Beloved," our "good
Friend," as St. Teresa of Avila tells us. There is a shade
of difference between these two loves. The former is necessarily secret, deeper and more impassioned. Through it our
Lord Jesus Christ is first served, first loved. It is a more
abandoned love, in which the whole soul gives itself, consecrates itself, becomes fused in God, pledges itself, is

immolated. The latter is a calmer, more tranquil love that
does not demand the total conquest of self as does the first.
It is more like the exchange of glances between friends as
they work together.

The virtue of obedience. This is the most difficult and
important of the three, although poverty remains first,
indispensable. Obedience consists in surrendering our will
to God, and in doing His will in all things. To this end,
we submit our actions to the judgment of God's representative, His image, His legitimate envoy. Making a vow of
obedience merely strengthens and confirms our voluntary
and very meritorious effort. This is particularly true in
an era when the individual's self-determination is considered an absolute, inalienable right, and when any sacrifice
of this nature is extremely painful.

The practice of obedience is conceivable either in terms
of a "rule" which interprets authoritatively and with ecclesiastical approbation a certain number of details, habits, left
to the free choice of the individual by the Commandments
of God (such a "rule" specifies practices, controls, and pro-
hibitions); or obedience may be practiced within the frame-
work of a "living rule," with reference to a particular person who is considered God's representative by legitimate
delegation.

Obedience to a person presupposes, or better still, demands a real spirit of faith. If we do not see God's will in
this person's commands, we no longer have religious obedience but only servile submission or a sentimental subordination. These are a far cry from the virtue of obedience, and are neither meritorious nor sanctifying. But
if we see God in the person of the one who commands, we
maintain our soul in great peace, and the inevitable faults
of our superior (faults that are sometimes quite glaring)
do not disturb us. Thus we can sanctify that part of us
that is noblest and most difficult to bend, namely, our free

will, by submitting it deliberately and with a supernatural attitude.

Let us never forget that Christ became "obedient to death, even to death on a cross" (Phil. 2:8). Finally let us remember that these three virtues, which seem restrictive at first glance, are not so much burdens as wings. Poverty brings us through affective or effective privation to the possession of the only Good that is worthy of our desire. Chastity introduces us to infinite Love. Obedience makes us subject to God only in order to ennoble and fecundate our action. "Take this short and perfect word: Forsake all and thou shalt find all. . . ."

Fraternal Charity

The Gospel tells us: "Thou shalt love thy neighbor as thyself." And the parable of the Good Samaritan shows us the scope of the word "neighbor." But since this subject is immense, let us limit ourselves to a meditation on the marks that the Holy Spirit usually impresses upon the hearts of those of us who are docile to Him, with regard to our really close neighbors: relatives, colleagues and friends, children, and most particularly those who share our life, our apostolic desires, our duties of state.

Negatively, the Holy Spirit inspires us not to judge them: Judge not! The implication is: do not judge unfavorably like a stern judge who is proud of his innocence, full of his own superiority. Such a one was Pilate, who said to Our Lord: "Dost thou not speak to me? Dost thou not know that I have power to crucify thee, and that I have power to release thee?" (John 19:10). Let us not drag before the tribunal of our mind, like a pitiful handcuffed prisoner, the person or the behavior of our brothers, our rivals, even of our adversaries.

It may be one of our superiors. We preserve formalities, we show deference, but deep within us we condemn: "Here is a superior person, very intelligent, but unfit to handle practical matters, unable to see through situations, full of himself, etc."

Or it may be one of our equals. We plead bitterly the case of aggravating circumstances: "Always full of petty schemes, lacking in consideration, having excessive simplicity or perhaps affected simplicity, extreme sensitiveness; a snob, overrated talent, makes everything revolve around himself . . . full of imaginary ailments, always pampering himself . . . never keeps his promises, etc."

Very different is the rule inspired by the Holy Spirit: if you cannot judge favorably, do not judge. If you cannot save the acts, then save the intentions. "Even if an action had a hundred faces, he would choose the most favorable" (St. Francis de Sales). And that is possible, without any sleight of hand or subtle casuistry. It is often no more than justice! Let us place ourselves in our neighbor's place. Would I want to be judged so rigorously? Have I deserved to be treated so harshly in such and such a case? Am I worth more than you, poor brother whom I condemn? And if so, is it due to the grace of God or to the victories of my own courage? There are roots of pharisaism here that need to be ripped out: "I am not like the rest of men!" (Luke 18:11).

On the positive side, the Holy Spirit inspires *universal* charity. I must love all my companions, although it would be impossible and chimerical to want to love them all equally. I must love all men: "Love your enemies." What, then, of our brothers? Therefore, let us make no exceptions, let us not look upon anyone as a black sheep. Just preferences are permissible of course, based on gratitude, on services received or returned, on spiritual helpfulness. And it will always be easier, more pleasant to establish a rapport with some than with others. But this should take nothing away from our charity for the others. Above all, we must love the sick, those who are weakest, the most abandoned or unhappy, those who are troubled, tempted. . . .

The Holy Spirit also inspires a charity that is sincere and effective. *Sincere* charity, as between brothers and sisters who love one another deeply without mentioning it often. It is all quite natural. No affectation, no whispered secrets, no clandestine ways. Brothers are happy to be together, even when they are not talking. They are happy to work together. They share everything, some doing what the others cannot do and finding it quite natural to sacrifice themselves for them. Now this demands humility, hence humiliation, hence courage. Let no one say: I cannot do it. I am cold, distant. You can be more amiable. Let your treasure shine forth. It may not be very great, but no one is asking more of you than what you have to give.

Secondly, the Holy Spirit inspires *effective* love, not in words but in acts, in the simple and fraternal communication of whatever good we possess: our small talents, our skills, our self-sacrifice, our learning, our devotion and piety, our wit, our cheerfulness, our good will (this latter being the resource of those who have few others). Make your brothers benefit from the good within you. Pray for them, suffer for them. We truly love only those for whom we have suffered.

Finally, this love is *respectful,* because all men have been redeemed: "For you have been bought at a great price" (1 Cor. 6:20). It is respectful also because you are all in the service of the King. St. Clare, as superior and mistress of novices, considered herself "the governess of the daughters of the great King."

Suggested Reading

The Gospel according to St. John, Chapter 13.

The Imitation of Christ, Book III, Chapters 32, 34, and 37.

Take this short and perfect word: Forsake all and thou shalt find all. . . . Lord, this is no one-day's work, no child's play . . . . Son, thou must not be turned back, nor presently cast down, when thou hearest what the way of the perfect is: but rather be incited thereby to undertake great things, or at least to sigh after them with an earnest desire (*The Imitation of Christ,* Book III, Chapter 32, 1-3).

But above all these things have charity, which is the bond of perfection. And may the peace of Christ reign in your hearts; unto that peace, indeed, you were called in one body (Col. 3:14-15).

Put on therefore, as God's chosen ones, holy and beloved, a heart of mercy, kindness, humility, meekness, patience. Bear with one another and forgive one another, ... even as the Lord has forgiven you, so also do you forgive (Col. 3:12-13).

He [our Lord] loves those who love Him. And what a Beloved, what a good Friend He is! (St. Teresa of Avila).

II

THE PASSION OF OUR LORD

1.

The Law of Charity and of Service (Gospel of St. John, Chapter 13)

Let us ask God to grant us a love for great duties and disgust for our own infidelities.

What great duties? Service and charity after the example of Jesus Christ. We are Christians, His disciples. Well, "no servant is greater than his master" (John 15:20). If we want to serve God, we must learn from Christ, we must be conformable to Him. The episode of the washing of the feet (John 13:1 ff.) which opens the Passion is of capital importance because it gives us an example, a decisive lesson: "For I have given you an example, that as I have done to you, so you also should do" (John 13:15).

Let us inquire into the conditions of this service.

Christ was perfectly aware of His condition, and of the conditions of His service. He did not obey unthinking instinct. He knew what He was, that He had come forth from His Father and that He would return to Him. He knew what His disciples were worth: "You are clean, but not all" (John 13:10). He knew that even the others would

abandon Him within three hours. He knew He was Master
and Lord: "You call me Master and Lord. . . ." (John
13:13). It was under such conditions that He loved: "having loved his own who were in the world, [he] loved them
to the end" (John 13:1).

So too, we must open our eyes to the true light. We
must remember who God is and what we are. He exists
in Himself and of Himself. He owes nothing to anyone.
Out of His goodness He creates, He wants to bring into
being happy, responsible creatures. We come from Him.
We owe Him everything. We have nothing by which we
can explain ourselves, nothing that will satisfy us, nor
suffice us. Everything within us, even that by which we
offend Him, comes from God: primordial Goodness. All
our desires, even our evil ones, tend toward Him in principle: final Goodness.

Under these conditions of singular lucidity, of veritable
clairvoyance, Jesus served His brothers. He served them
in humility, as a slave, a servant. He served them without
preference: Peter, John, Judas. . . . Without demanding
any reward. In a spirit of love and total dedication, seeing
God His Father in them. He said "I will serve!" and thus
closed and healed the great wound from which the lifeblood
of humanity flows, the wound of pride, independence, egoism, self-determination, living for self.

As creatures, as Christians, we already owe our lives
to the service of God and of our brothers. But we have
received a special call. Jesus wants us closer to Him, He
wants us to be sharers in His apostolate, disciples, co-re-
deemers, associates in His work, an army on the offensive
against pride. And thus the service that we all owe takes
on for us a new and twofold character: it is more constrain-
ing. It is no longer merely a condition, but the essential
of our life. It is not only the work of justice, of obedience
to the great law of submission, but a work of love freely
given, freely carried to heroism. A son helps his parents if
he provides for their livelihood. But if he goes beyond that

and becomes their mainstay, their hands, their eyes, their guide, what a difference! Our call to service is of this second sort.

Serviam, Domine, tecum. Lord, I will serve, with Thee!

Jesus the Ransom and Victim of Sin (Mark 14:32-52)

The main obstacle, the only obstacle to God's service within us and outside of us is sin. The only real evil is sin, that is, willful moral deviation, deliberate withdrawal of our actions from God's known will, the substitution of our egoism, of our sensual and proud self for the worship of God. It is Lucifer's cry: "I will not serve!"

In the Garden of Olives, Jesus measured Himself against sin, that formidable adversary. He entered into agony, but triumphed over His enemy. He fought, not with His divine strength, but in His strictly human condition, a condition that was terrifyingly, cruelly human, a condition of fear, weariness, sadness: "and he began to feel dread and to be exceedingly troubled" (Mark 14:33).

How could that be? Because Jesus had to pay for the sins of the world. "Behold, the lamb of God, who takes away the sin of the world!" (John 1:29). "[He] was delivered up for our sins" (Rom. 4:25). "[He] gave himself for our sins" (Gal. 1:4). "Who himself bore our sins in his body" (1 Pet. 2:24). "For our sakes [God] made him to be sin who knew nothing of sin. . . ." (2 Cor. 5:21).

Jesus freely accepted this role, this function, as a guarantee, as a victim of expiation, a ransom, a substitute, for sinners: "Sacrifices and oblations and holocausts and sin-offerings thou wouldst not . . . and then [I said] 'behold, I come to do thy will, O God' " (Heb. 10:8-9). He accepted this will without hesitation, totally.

God the Father accepted Him also. And behold, the chalice before the Victim: "Shall I not drink the cup that the Father has given me?" (John 18:11).

But no! There was horror, revulsion, excruciating

agony: "Father . . . Remove this cup from me" (Mark
14:36). "Father, all things are possible to thee" (ibid).
Remove! Why? Because the cup is too bitter, because it
is too abominable; because it contains all hypocrisy, all
lewdness, all pride, all cruelty, all debauchery, all scandal,
all calumny, all injustice, all aversion, all sensuality, all
sinful pleasure, all murders, all robberies, all crimes, all
blasphemies, all forgetting of God, all omissions, all negligences. The sins of a life! What terrible disclosures there
can be after one reaches the age of forty! One can't remember any more. And this applies to an ordinary man,
not a notorious criminal. But now, it is too much! Remove. . . .

And yet: "not what I will, but what thou willest" (Mark
14:36) " . . . he fell on the ground, and began to pray"
(Mark 14:35).

Jesus, I want to help you too. I want to be with you.

Wait a minute! Are you worthy? On whose side are
you? On the side of the Victim? Dare to say so. No, you
won't say it. You did not see deep into the cup. At the
bottom lie also the sins of the good, the sins of friends, the
weaknesses, negligences, perfidies, and cowardly actions
that you call your "little sins." But coming from you after
so many graces!

The roots of evil are still within us: self-love, egoism
that stains everything, makes everything a matter of self-
interest, of private concern; lies, insincerity, indiscretions,
vanity; our inability to take any pleasure in what is good,
and our great pleasure in evil, in what is less good. Then
there are our rejections of grace, our excesses, our negligences. And all this from friends, servants, apostles.

"Against thee . . . have I sinned and, what is evil in thy
sight, I have done" (Ps. 50:5). "Behold, I was born in
iniquity, and in sin did my mother conceive me" (Ps. 50:7).
The root of sin. . . .

And yet I must be the enemy of sin, the destroyer of sin. I must be on Jesus' side! Wash me still more from my sins!

Suggested Reading

The Imitation of Christ, Book I, Chapter 6; Book III, Chapters 1, 2, and 3.

Psalms 31, 41, 50, and 54.

2.

The Passion of the Flesh

We shall meditate upon the passion of the flesh in two episodes: one that exemplifies improvised brutality (Mark 14:65), and another that consists in organized and concerted torture (Mark 15:15).

The necessity of two kinds of penance:

a) The penance that comes to us by way of Providence, without our desiring it, being attracted to it, or asking for it. That is the principal kind of penance, that is "the cross." It includes trials in matters of health and all that follows from them: precautions, sufferings, forced rest; the ordeal of uninterrupted work that is tedious, compulsory, lacking interest; the hardships and discomforts of travel, etc.; trials of the spiritual life: dryness, boredom, disgust, temptations.

b) The penance that is freely chosen and that varies according to our inclinations and capacities. Mortification of our curiosity; living a hard and laborious life, a simple but not a slipshod life, a sober life, not one of great deprivations. This is penance in the strict sense, and it is necessary. But it calls for the discretion of obedience.

First episode: "Then [the members of the Sanhedrin] spat in his face and buffeted him; while others struck his face with the palms of their hands, saying, 'Prophesy to us,

O Christ! who is that struck thee?' " (Matt. 26:67-68).
Everybody wants to have a part in it and they let themselves go to their hearts' content. This is brutality and
derision. The blows of life: bitter disappointments. The
blows of men: ingratitude, the requiting of good with
evil. The blows of Satan: temptations.

Second episode: "But Jesus he scourged and delivered
to be crucified" (Mark 15:15). This was real torture, in-
volving deliberate preparation, nakedness, shackles, cruel
blows given with instruments that either lashed, or slashed,
or crushed. Pilate's purpose demanded that this punishment be inflicted in its full rigor; and it was inflicted in
true Roman fashion by Romans who were experts in this
mode of torture.

Our Lord really suffered, for He was a perfect man
endowed with great sensibility and delicacy: He was subject to shame, He was keenly sensitive to the brutality, to
the loathsome taunts, to the blows.

The Prophet's vision: a leper! "From the sole of the
foot unto the top of the head, there is no soundness therein"
(Is. 1:6).

The Silence of Jesus

Matt. 26:59-63. Before the accusations of the false wit-
nesses, *Jesus kept silence.*

Matt. 27:11-14. Before Pilate who was interested and
inclined to take a favorable view and before those who
accused Him, Jesus "did not answer him a single word, so
that the procurator wondered exceedingly."

Luke 23:8-11. Before Herod who "put many questions
to him," Jesus made no answer.

In this context we must consider *the wound of words.*
Words of others that wound us. My words: evil, unkind,
cruel — "sharp arrows . . . and intense fire" (Ps. 119:4).
The sword of the tongue can kill. My words: vain, insincere, worldly, too free; useless, empty, distracting; indis-

creet — secrets betrayed, sins of others needlessly revealed, improper disclosures, reporting to others what has been said about them (diabolical!).

Salutary silence. The silence of reserve: a great force in education and in everyday life. The silence of recollection: avoids sins, fecundates the interior life, both spiritual and intellectual, increases our work output. The silence of charity: meritorious and generous. The silence of humility: we should not defend ourselves when there is no serious reason for doing so. We should not tell all we know, and we should say nothing of what we do not know or know only imperfectly.

The silence of Jesus before His impassioned, unjust, persistent accusers; before those who could have comforted and defended Him if He Himself had agreed to betray His mission, to condescend to their whims. And this silence was broken only for solid reasons of charity, of the apostolate, of bearing witness to the Truth.

Suggested Reading

The Imitation of Christ, Book I, Chapter 10; Book II, Chapters 6, 7, and 8.

Psalms 72, 76.

3.

The Passion and the Sensibilities of Jesus

This most important aspect of the Passion cannot be summed up in a single episode, for the whole of the Passion gives us an important lesson on this point — a lesson in self-forgetfulness and self-giving, amid and notwithstanding the most terrible sufferings of sensibilities tested to their utmost capacity for endurance.

Let us first of all try to visualize the sufferings of our Lord's sensibilities:

With regard to men: His apostles in flight, dispersed —
Peter, Judas; His Mother suffering anguish beyond words;
His enemies in insolent, brutal triumph; His people crying
out: "His blood be on us and on our children" (Matt. 27:25).

With regard to Himself: His contact with coarse, evil,
ungrateful, unjust men; His exhaustion from His agony,
His shackles, His opprobrium, His tortures; the clear vision
of what yet awaited Him; the absence of all consolation
either from earth or from heaven.

In this state "Christ did not please himself" (Rom. 15:
3). He forgot Himself, He gave Himself, He lived for
others. There was no self-pity. He thought of others. Of
the executioners: "Father, forgive them" (Luke 23:34).
Of the daughters of Jerusalem: "Do not weep for me, but
weep for yourselves" (Luke 23:28). Of the good thief:
"This day thou shalt be with me in paradise" (Luke 23:
43). Of His Mother: "Behold, thy mother" (John 19:27).
Of His mission: "This is why I . . . have come into the world,
to bear witness to the truth. Everyone who is of the truth
hears my voice" (John 18:37).

Our sensibilities are very different from those of our
Lord's. The fact remains that in imitation of Him and with
His help we must master them. But how?

By controlling and mortifying them. No childishness.
No overly human affection. St. Teresa of Avila wanted her
Carmelites to have virile souls. Likewise, we must ac-
custom ourselves not to demand or to give manifestations
of unduly sensible affection.

By dominating them through prayer, diversion, self-
forgetfulness, abnegation, self-giving. That is sometimes
heroic, and always necessary. On the contrary, the more
we surrender to our sensibilities, the more demanding they
are. The more we think on our vexations, the worse they
get; the less attention we give them, the stronger we become. The more we give, the more we receive.

By submitting to whomever has the mission to guide us, for in moments of uncertainty we cannot see clearly. "This is your hour, and the power of darkness" (Luke 22: 53). Then amid the storm and the darkness a beacon still shines: obedience. An anchor still holds: our duty of state. We still have a steadfast hope of salvation: "I know whom I have believed" (2 Tim. 1:12).

By following the example of Jesus: "Have this mind in you which was also in Christ Jesus" (Phil. 2:5). "If you want to come after me, deny yourself, and take up your cross and follow me" (cf. Luke 9:23).

The Passion of Honor (Matt. 27: 26-33; Luke 23:5-12.)

The appearance before Herod. Here the shame consists in the scorn of the men of the world for all that is above them or that condemns them. Hence their disdain for any great work to be done — disinterested work, sincere, deeply Christian, supernatural work.

The world treats all apostles as it did Jesus: "But Herod . . . mocked him, arraying him in a bright robe" (Luke 23:11). It treats them as dreamers, visionaries, or else it suspects their disinterestedness.

Jesus was completely silent before Herod. This is the only episode of the Passion when He said nothing! For in this man He found no reflection of the Father: no legitimate authority, no genuine desire for truth. There was no way He could help him. He wanted to have nothing to do with deceivers, triflers. Well, this scorn of the world is indispensable and sanctifying for apostles, Jesus' friends, who are learning to climb the steep path of spiritual progress.

The scene of organized derision. It was cruel and disgraceful. The entire cohort gathered. Jesus was stripped again, then mockingly attired like a king in a play; a crown, a royal cloak, a scepter. Derisive honors, cruel games.

The head of Jesus, a king crowned with thorns. On

this point, meditate on the spirit of pride, of independence
that is the mark of our times, especially among women.
Everyone wants to be the master: I will not serve! I will
not believe! The arguments are almost all based on
authority usurped from God Himself — usurped above all
from His legitimate representatives: ecclesiastical leaders,
spiritual directors, superiors, those in positions of professional responsibility.

It is of utmost importance that we combat this trend.
We must fight it within ourselves by intelligent and willing
submission; and fight it outside of us by reminding others
of the eternal laws, of man's initial and never-ending dependence; by showing them the ridiculous impotence of the
idol "self," its proven incapacity to bring us into being or to
maintain and perfect us in being, its total inability to im-
prove us, to beatify us; by pointing to the sterility of pride,
of stubborn refusal to understand.

Jesus, King!

Suggested Reading

The Imitation of Christ, Book III, Chapters 27, 32, and 37.
Psalms 21 and 37.

4.

The Death of Jesus   (John 19:23-30.)

The dividing of the garments: Jesus wants to keep
nothing for Himself. At Bethlehem He had swaddling
clothes. On the Cross, He is naked and wills that His
garments be taken from Him. "Naked, I shall follow the
naked Jesus." Affective detachment must be all the greater
in the measure that the sword of religious poverty does not
strike the blow of immolation.

The seamless tunic, woven by the Blessed Virgin. It is
the symbol of integral, orthodox, total faith, a faith that
does not pick and choose, that cleaves to God's Revelation.

(One of our principal purposes, in fact the chief purpose of our Society[1] is to preserve and inculcate this Revelation.) "For I betrothed you to one spouse, that I might present you a chaste virgin to Christ" (2 Cor. 11:2). The symbol of our pledged faith in Christ.

Mary bequeathed to St. John, and John's acceptance. Our devotion to Mary should be filial, simple, trusting, tender. Let us remember that in general we have to ask for devotion: "Take away my stony heart and give me a heart of flesh" (cf. Ezech. 11:19). We must give devotion to Mary a place of honor, and favor it within the context of our other devotions. We should look upon it as a means of safeguarding the great Christian virtues of faith, charity, simplicity, work, obedience, and submission to God.

I thirst, in the strict sense: "He gave a Man to men." In the figurative sense: zeal for souls.

"It is consummated!" The meaning and the goal of life is death with Jesus. What a consolation to be able to say: "I have accomplished the work that thou hast given me to do" (John 17:4). Not the work that I have chosen, but the one that your Providence has assigned to me. I have done it to the end.

The Sacred Heart

In thinking of Jesus' love for us, let us call to mind its prodigious *disinterestedness:* "He has first loved us" (1 John 4:10). "Christ . . . died . . . for sins, the Just for the unjust" (1 Pet. 3:18). "Do good . . . not hoping for any return" (Luke 6:35). "I am your Friend even more than this one and that one."

Its *efficacy:* "Physicians will not save you, for you will die in the end." Jesus' love saves us from eternal damnation and wins eternal love for us. It obtains for us an

---

[1] The Daughters of St. Francis Xavier, founded by Father de Grandmaison. (Tr.)

infinite power for reparation, for innocence preserved or regained.

Its *sweetness:* It is a human love, but one that is all-pure (free from any sting of concupiscence, without any bitter aftertaste or dregs, without any disillusioned to-morrow). It is a jealous love, but it is not exclusive. It is enduring and the pledge of hope: "and your joy no one shall take from you" (John 16:22). It is a love that bears within itself the seeds of a sweetness that is everlasting, beatifying, divine. And this love is a source of joy for us here and now.

Let us live for the One who died for us.

Suggested Reading

The Imitation of Christ, Book II, Chapter 11; Book III, Chapters 21 and 22.

Psalms 83 and 131.

III

OUR LIFE HIDDEN IN GOD

1.

The Death of Sin

St. Paul always pictures Christian life as a death followed by a resurrection: "For you have died and your life is hidden with Christ in God" (Col. 3:3). "Thus do you consider yourselves also as dead to sin, but alive to God in Christ Jesus" (Rom. 6:11). "For we were buried with [Christ] . . . . so we also may walk in newness of life" (Rom. 6:4).

Adopting this view of faith, we shall meditate successively on death to sin and then on the new life modeled on Christ's by which we become new creatures, new men "conformable" to Christ.

Our concern is to reform our lives, to renew ourselves, to die still more to sin, for there are dead men that still need to be killed. While Baptism dealt a virtually mortal blow to our "old man," it did not annihilate him. The tree trunk clings to life although the ax is deep in its roots. It can still grow back, multiply again in evil acts that are too human, too natural. And these revivals can choke off the graft of the good tree. They can kill the new, risen man, or at least greatly lessen his resemblance to Christ, and hence his apostolic efficacy.

Let us meditate on the fact that we are sinners, that the old man still lives within us either through habitual sins in the strict sense, through sinful habits, or through vestiges of sin and inclinations to evil which are the fruit of our corrupted or unbalanced temperament. The latter may be the consequences of vices to which we have personally consented in the past, or simply the vices of our forefathers that we have inherited. Included in this second category are involuntary faults, simple defects, or predispositions to evil. All these things are components of "the flesh," of "the old man," of sin — whether original or actual.

After having asked our Lord to enlighten us in this painful meditation, we shall reflect on our *habitual voluntary sins*. These can be classified under the various forms of egoism: proud, arrogant, self-sufficient, vain egoism; and sensual, overly sensitive, lazy, indolent egoism.

To sins of pride belong all our desires to try to cut a figure, our strategies to push ourselves forward: ostentation, lying, trifling excuses, exaggerations, indiscretions intended to show that we know more than we are telling; refusals to admit our faults, stubbornness, obstinacy, impatience, ruffled self-love, voluntary anxiety; harshness in words, in judgments, lack of charity either through frivolity or through a sentiment of partiality.

Sins of sensuality include all that is related to sloth, negligence, gluttony, excessive affection, uncontrolled imagination, random reading, daydreams, weakness of will, discouragement, jealousy and envy, the omission of the good we should do, resistance to grace, fear of goodness.

Let us now consider our *faults,* our predispositions to evil. What a sad sight! It is like a country ravaged by enemy troops. Almost all of our faculties are darkened, damaged.

Our intellect is frivolous, incapable of prolonged attention. It judges too quickly, too severely; it is superficial, narrow. "No one has any sense except us and our friends."

Our will is feeble, acting by fits and starts. Now it is weak, yielding to evil influences, to vain, stubborn dissipation. Again it is obstinate and hard, closed to all goodness; or intemperate, capricious.

Our imagination reviews again all that arouses our anger, indignation, discouragement, sadness, melancholy. It exaggerates everything, making us live in a fanciful and unreal world.

Our sensibilities are obtuse and cold, incapable of generous self-giving; or else they are all aquiver and overly passionate. We tend to make a tragedy out of everything that happens to us. We allow our emotions to be extreme in their manifestations, indiscreet in their demands, badly controlled or uncontrolled. We act like spoiled children.

Such is the sad spectacle of the self without God, of the self that has not risen again or been refashioned in the image of Christ, transformed by His grace, configured to the Lord Jesus.

Let us strive to see our faults clearly.

Death to Sin

The death of the "old man," of the carnal, natural, evil man, death to sin, consists, insofar as we are concerned, in clearly realizing the malice of sin and of detaching ourselves from it. (This does not imply that we are to forget the indispensable and preponderant role of grace. For we have the right and the duty to believe that grace will never fail to sustain our good will and make it efficacious, since it is grace that in the first place inspires our will to goodness.)

The malice of sin and of the evil inclinations which we

mentioned above is very great indeed. And yet we are
immunized, so to speak, against a clear, piercing, efficacious
view of this evil. We must therefore pray for light. Mean-
while, we can make comparisons, and consider the consequences of sin. On this point St. Ignatius invites us to
meditate upon a few archetypal sins that allow us to judge
the tree by its fruits: the sin of the angel, the sin of the
first man, personal sin.

Sin is serious in its aftereffects and consequences. But
it is serious also in itself, because it overthrows the natural
and divine order of things, it disrupts the most fundamental
relationships between the Creator and His creatures. It
disjoints us, disorients us. It deprives God of honor and
glory to the extent that such a thing is possible. It robs
the Blood of Jesus Christ of its efficacy. It places us in
danger of damnation and of forfeiting the goal of our life.

Suggested Reading

The Imitation of Christ, Book I, Chapters 2, 7, and 11;
Book II, Chapter 1.

Psalms 39 and 50.

For how shall we who are dead to sin still live in it? . . .
Thus do you consider yourselves also as dead to sin, but alive
to God in Christ Jesus (Rom. 6:2, 11).

2.

The Risen Life with Christ

Death to sin, to evil, must be continually renewed in the
full measure that evil, sin, strives and succeeds in insinuat-
ing itself once more into our soul. Habitual vigilance and
ordinary wisdom suffice to safeguard the renewed effort we
make from time to time through a more complete purification.

But we want to die only in order to live more fully.
We want to die only in order to rise again. Well, the form

of this resurrection does not depend on our efforts, our meditations, our preferences. It has a clearly defined Model who is also the impelling force and agent of this resurrection, and this Model is Jesus Christ.

We must rise again with Him. Jesus is the impelling power and perfect Exemplar of this new, restored, rejuvenated life. We shall meditate upon the sense in which He is our Model, but, for the present, let us see how He is the inmost power of our moral and religious reformation.

As Master and Teacher, He is the interior force of our new life. This is His role in His Gospel and in His teaching Church. We must renew, nourish, and enlighten our faith now more than ever, so that this faith may become a beautiful flame, pure, illuminating, contagious. "As the lamp shining . . ." (Ecclus. 26:22). "You call me Master and Lord, and you say well, for so I am" (John 13:13).

It follows that we are not to accept any other human master, whoever he may be, regardless of the current vogue or the urging of others. It follows that we must not neglect our religious instruction, our study of the catechism, etc. It follows that we must pray often to increase our faith: "I do believe [Lord]; help my unbelief" (Mark 9:23).

He is also our strength as our *Savior*. We always need to be saved, washed, purified. Well, Jesus is there: "Behold, the lamb of God, who takes away the sins of the world!" (John 1:29). He is there in the priest's absolution, He is there in the cross. We must never say to ourselves that we have sinned too much, for Jesus is our Savior. He is Supreme Mercy. We need to be forgiven, to find a supreme mercy.

He is our strength as our *Friend,* our companion, the center of our hearts. We must live *in Christo Jesu,* as in an enveloping atmosphere, a place of rest, a haven of peace and grace, a family gathering-place, warm and affable. How can we do it? Through Holy Communion that unites us to Him in very truth; by the habitual offering and

decision to please Him above all else, to sacrifice everything
to Him, to love Him with a love of preference, of predilection, of absolute abandonment, for time and eternity:
"Tu solus Sanctus, Tu solus Dominus, Tu solus Altissimus."

Let us love other things and other people: those who
are suffering, the saints, the poor, those near and dear to us
(our family, our companions, our friends). But let us love
them *in Christo Jesu,* in this divine atmosphere. Then "our
conversation [will be] in heaven" (Phil. 3:20). The worth
of any meditation, prayer, sacrifice, zeal, and apostolate is
measured by the degree to which it unites and configures
us to Him.

> In the darkest night and in agony, He is there.
> In suffering and humiliation, He is even closer.
> In absences and losses, He is still there.
> At the hour of death, He is always there.

Putting on Christ

To put on Christ, we must imitate Him, take Him as
our Model. In what ways? St. Paul gives us the answer:
"Have this mind in you which was also in Christ Jesus, who
though he was by nature God . . . emptied himself, taking
the nature of a slave and . . . . humbled himself, becoming obedient to death, even to death on a cross" (Phil.
2:5-8).

Therefore, we must conform ourselves fundamentally to
Christ by abnegation to the point of emptying ourselves
completely of self: "He emptied himself." Jesus deliberately renounced the infinite honors that were due Him
as Son of God equal to the Father and accepted the form
of a slave, the condition of a slave, carrying humility and
obedience to their ultimate expression, even to death, the
death of the Cross.

We must resign ourselves to serve: "taking the nature
of a slave." "To serve" is our motto. But there are all
kinds of service. There is glorious service that is rewarded

and brilliant, and there is humble service that is exhausting, hard, servile, persevering. There is the service of a handsome soldier and the service of a slave. We must have the spirit of the soldier and the abnegation of the slave. We must do the work of a slave with the soul of a hero. Such was the service of Christ.

But it is so hard! It includes the acceptance of work that is never praised or noticed, and self-sacrifice that is sometimes misunderstood. If we were always understood when we tried to do good, we would be serving to please men and we would have our reward here on earth. How many men did Jesus serve without being recognized? How many does He save who do not know Him and who will only realize in heaven that they owe everything to Him.

"He humbled himself, becoming obedient to death, even to death on a cross" (Phil. 2:8). Obedience, submission is humiliating, especially when it consists in accepting reproaches, rebukes, admonitions, and directions. To obey always means to humble oneself. And often the best way of humbling oneself is by obeying one's rule, one's superior, and so on. Jesus obeyed to death. Now, this is frequently the case in the Army, and a daily occurrence in wartime. But He obeyed even to death on a Cross. Here we lack terms of comparison. Our service could not possibly go that far. And yet it is good for us to be inspired by this spectacle that we can imitate only in a remote way. On the other hand our service does sometimes involve sacrifices. We may be asked to forego a certain honor, to give up the companionship of old friends, to leave familiar surroundings: *mortem autem crucis.*

Jesus kept advancing in the path of pure service, of humble, naked service totally devoid of honor and rewards. He went as far as accepting the betrayal of Judas, the abandonment of those nearest to Him, Peter's denial, His enemies' triumphant persecution, apparent abandonment by His own Father: *mortem autem Crucis.*

We must enter into this spirit at all costs if we want to serve God seriously and to put on Jesus Christ. Otherwise it is a comedy, and a brutal one. When we serve to the end and make sacrifices without reservation, keeping nothing for ourselves, we find true merit and joy, we find the savor of Jesus.

Let us see therefore what obstacles there are within us, whether of sentiment or character, of cowardice or egoism, that hinder us from this service.

O Mary, introduce us into the spirit of Jesus. You who clothed Him so many times when He was little, clothe us now in His tastes, His preferences, His wishes.

Mary, Guardian and Model of our Life Hidden with Christ in God

Mary was the model of this life. It is written of her that she "kept all these things carefully in her heart" (Luke 2:51). That is to say, she meditated lovingly upon all the mysteries of the childhood, the hidden and public life, the suffering and glorious life of her Son. To put it another way, she kept Him constantly present in her mind and heart.

The Gospel points to the fact that Mary lived a simple, ordinary life, outwardly devoid of grandeur. This was fitting for one who was to be the model for all, not merely for a single class of people or a select few. But this hidden life is the one we must lead under circumstances that demand it of us.

Mary is the guardian of our life hidden with Christ in God: because she is our Mother and will give us the confidence to dare to believe in the great and unbelievable friendship of our Lord and God; because through her we shall win victories over our faults and forgiveness for our sins that we would sometimes be too much ashamed to ask of our Lord; because we are profoundly devoted and consecrated to her, and our very wretchedness calls forth her great compassion and Mother's love.

Suggested Reading

The Imitation of Christ, Book II, Chapters 7 and 8; Book III, Chapter 10.

Psalms 83 and 91.

. . . that, just as Christ has arisen from the dead through the glory of the Father, so we also may walk in newness of life (Rom. 6:4).

Have this mind in you which was also in Christ Jesus, who though he was by nature God . . . emptied himself, taking the nature of a slave and . . . . humbled himself, becoming obedient to death, even to death on a cross (Phil. 2:5-8).

Learn from me, for I am meek and humble of heart (Matt. 11:29).

3.

Our Life Hidden with Christ in God. "For you have died and your life is hidden with Christ in God" (Col. 3:3).

A hidden life: True, nothing has changed outwardly, there is no exterior brilliance. In fact, quite the contrary! There is more subordination, more humility, more obscurity. There is less "living one's own life," a less vivid personality. But there is more life, for to live is to think, to delight in the truth. To live is to love and to act. And in such a life we shall have more truth: a clearer view of the eternal order of things, a more accurate evaluation of what is fundamental and of prime importance. We shall realize that all the rest is simply literature, that is, a matter of opinions, ephemeral shadows, darkness.

We shall love more because our hearts will be possessed by a great love. As one young religious used to say: "Every day is a feast day for me, the feast of our immortal love!" [1] Other loves pass, die, or vanish, falling from their own weakness. And from our love of God we shall draw reserves of tenderness and efficacious self-giving for our fellow men.

---

[1] Brother Léon Besnardeau, S.J.

We shall also act with greater efficacy because we shall be working with eternal materials, we shall be weaving on the imperishable warp of human souls.

Hidden with Christ in God. Let us return to this point of utmost importance. It involves a serious difficulty, namely this: we do not dare to believe in it or try it, because it is too beautiful to be true. *Cum Christo!* Is it possible that I, a speck of nothingness, can have friendly converse with the Word of God, with infinite Wisdom? Is it possible that I can love Him! *In Deo.* . . . Indeed! Can I really love Him in a divine atmosphere, I who am intimidated by a public figure, who would not dare speak to certain people? I who am destitute of all goodness?

The answer is "Yes." It is our faith. "For God so loved the world that he gave his only-begotten Son, that those who believe in him may not perish, but may have life everlasting" (John 3:16). "I live in the faith of the Son of God, who loved me . . ." (Gal. 2:20). "I have loved thee with an everlasting love" (Jer. 31:3).

And then too, to love is to adore very efficaciously. For it means to submit our whole being to God at every single moment. It means to sing the hymn: "Divine Jesus, Supreme Mercy!" It means to give all for all.

The obstacle to such a life is our "self," our egoism, which finds this pure and healthful mountain air too rarefied for its free expansion, its vain dissipations, its pleasures, its tender self-concern, its eagerness for immediate sensual satisfactions, its oversensitivity to all that offends it. Thus our ego draws an opaque veil of anxiety between Jesus and us, a veil of unsound reasons, of feverish agitation, of wounded self-love. Once this obstacle, this veil, is cast aside, we can look at Jesus with the most tender respect, the most filial fear.

May my evil self perish, so that Jesus may live within me! "Christ did not please himself" (Rom. 15:3). If Jesus spared Himself, then let us spare ourselves. If Jesus has placed limitations upon His gift of Himself, then let us do likewise.

The Sweetness and Efficacy of This Life

This life, as we have said, is characterized by generous service, meekness, humility of heart, constant union with Jesus, and "obscurity" from the worldly and natural point of view.   And it is a *very sweet* life when we practice it seriously and generously.

It is sweet because so many thorns have been pulled out of our hearts: thorns of jealousy, pettiness, evil desires, selfishness, spite, wounded vanity, disordered affection, among others.

It is sweet because we walk in the light.   It matters not if this light is very pure and blessed, or cold, darkened by trials, cut through perhaps with clouds of temptation and doubt.   It still retains the power to show us our goal.   If it is not a lighthouse beacon, at least it is a tiny light that moves on before us: "a lantern for my feet" (Ps. 118:105).

It is sweet because we are proceeding in order, interiorly and exteriorly, we are proceeding in peace.   "And may the peace of [Christ] which surpasses all understanding guard your hearts and minds . . ." (Phil. 4:7).   Everything becomes a labor of love, including the Cross.

It is sweet because we walk in the company of brothers who love us and whom we love.   Temperaments sometimes clash, various traits may conflict: quickness versus slowness, intuition versus deduction, expansive feeling versus reserve, self-sacrifice that shines before the eyes of men versus hidden devotion.   But we love the same Master, we are laboring at the same task, we share the same treasure. We can count on our collective strength.   The devil can disturb this charity only by a willful complicity on our part. "A new commandment I give you, that you love one another" (John 13:34).

And moreover this life is *very efficacious* for good, because it is conformable to the life of Christ and therefore capable of transmitting His light (the *Lumen Christi* of Easter). It is capable of communicating His life by making others love it, capable of inculcating the taste and respect for what He loved: His Father, the salvation of souls, purity of heart, resigned trust, and abandonment.

It is efficacious because it is freed from all those harpoons of human, personal, selfish attachments that frustrate our apostolic efforts and render them sterile by making them consist entirely of external appearances.

It is efficacious because it makes us ready to undertake any kind of work, providing Jesus is served by it, including work that is lowly, unheroic. Great protectors are very fine, but it is the simple folk who love and serve. "O most merciful God, give us lowly protectors!"

It is efficacious because it fecundates, magnifies, raises up to the stars everyday and relatively easy actions. It makes them share in the infinite merits of Jesus, bathes them in His divine Blood, rendering them meritorious and redemptive.

It is efficacious because it keeps us joyful and enables us to lead others to love goodness and virtue, and sacrifice. "For we are the fragrance of Christ" (2 Cor. 2:15) in every place. The fragrant odor of certain islands can be detected far out to sea, long before they are seen (certain of the Antilles, and even Corsica).

Let us therefore die this blessed death so that we may live the new life with Christ, with God.

Note on Devotions

Desserts can be nourishing, too. This is the case with devotion in general and with "special" devotions. Of course there is greater need of devotion than of devotions.

Devotion nourishes us because it is a sweet and delicate poetry in our life, especially devotion to Mary.

It nourishes because it is a power, an efficacious and easy means of making us love God and divine things in our life. We learn by trying.

It nourishes because it is a humble path toward God's friendship, one that deifies even our body (St. Anthony of Padua's mule before the Blessed Sacrament).

It nourishes because it edifies others, and above all children.

But it must be a discreet, wise, unobtrusive devotion, that does not force itself on others, that does not publicize itself, in short, a simple devotion.

What devotions? All those that please us and that are beneficial, providing they are approved and spiritual: The Child Jesus, the Crucifix, the Hail Mary, the Holy Angels.

IV

CONFORMING OUR LIFE TO THE LIFE OF CHRIST

1.

The Fundamental Truth

The first of the exercises proposed by St. Ignatius consists in placing ourselves in the presence of the purpose of life. This is the fundamental truth, the truth that comes at the very beginning of every catechism.

We are alive, we have a certain capital in hand, whether great or small, five talents, two, or perhaps only one. We have a certain potential: intelligence, sensibilities, will and good will, inborn talents, acquired talents, learning, capacities, small talents; the gift of influencing others, enthusiasm, youth, health, years of experience; family, fortune (or lack of it); human hopes, ambitions, desires; divine gifts: piety, wisdom (a taste for divine things), virtues, etc.

All these things are in our hands in a certain measure and in a certain manner. What shall we do with them?

1) The solution to reject: use them for myself, appropriate them as my own. Strive to advance myself, to get rich, to enjoy myself. "Our lips are for us; who is Lord

over us?" (Ps. 11:5). In a word, to live my own life as I
please, according to my whims, for my own enjoyment.
To take as my rule, "Such is my good pleasure." This
solution is sadly lacking in realism, except for its malice
and for the beginning it makes in the direction of execu-
tion. But soon there will be disappointments, and all our
dreams will be bankrupt. The trifling pleasures we call to
our rescue will fill us with disgust, and leave us, as though
dying, in an immense void.

2) The solution of the man with one talent: bury my
treasure in the ground. Organize my life as if it were a
night journey in an uncomfortable day coach. Curl up, pad
myself; offer the least possible hold to dust, cold, suffering.
Refuse to do wrong, refuse to profess Nietzscheism or other
subversive doctrines, but arrange to suffer as little as
possible, give as little as possible of myself, work as little
as possible, serve as little as possible.

"Out of thy own mouth I judge thee, thou wicked servant" (Luke 19:22).

3) The right and realistic solution: make the most of
my talents, my capital, by praising and serving God. God
first served! "I am thine" (Ps. 118:94). "O Lord, I am
thy servant, and the son of thy handmaid" (Wisd. 9:5).

Why is this the right solution? Because it is founded
on truth. It is the practice of the First Commandment:
"Thou shalt love the Lord thy God with thy whole strength,
above all things." "The Lord thy God shalt thou adore,
and him only shalt thou serve."

God is primordial Goodness. All fatherhood comes from
Him. All created goodness is an outpouring of His super-
eminent Goodness, a defective imitation of His infinite
Being. We acknowledge this when we say: "O Lord, I am
thy servant." "We give thee thanks for thy great glory."

God is final Goodness: the end envisaged by every desire, the goal of all man's aspirations. He is the subsistent

God, without shadow, without deficiency, uneclipsed, without defect. He alone satisfies every hunger, He alone makes us holy: *Tu solus Sanctus, tu solus Dominus, tu solus Altissimus.*

We acknowledge it when we say: "I am Thine — to the depths, to the marrow of my being. I am Thine in all that I have, in all that I am, in all that I shall have, in all that I shall be. I am Thine in all that I cannot take from Thee (Providence, external circumstances). I am Thine in all that I might take from Thee (my own free choices)."

I am Thine. I cannot say: "I belong to *no one.*" That would be anarchy. Nor can I say: "I belong to *another.*" That would be slavery. Nor: "I am *my own.*" That would be egoism. I am Thine, O Lord, O Truth, O God!

The Will of God

"But blessed are your eyes, for they see; and your ears, for they hear. For amen I say to you, many prophets and just men have longed to see what you see, and they have not seen it; and to hear what you hear, and they have not heard it" (Matt. 13:16-17).

In his *Summa contra Gentiles,* St. Thomas points with emotion to the anxiety of the noblest minds of antiquity over the destiny of the human race. And to this he opposes the security of even the lowliest Christian. In the Middle Ages this security was a collective privilege, very generally enjoyed. Today it has again become rare. The words *I am Thine* contain everything we need.

This great truth has a practical and vitally important consequence. When we belong to God, we seek His will in all things, and then we do it in all things. Everything else will be given us besides.

Let us become deeply convinced of this consequence: I am Thine, therefore. . . . But it will all remain Platonic unless my actions, my operations, my will, my sensibilities

are impregnated with the will of God, unless they are
poured into the mold of His will. One goal and one alone
is necessary, indispensable: the service of God. One means
and one alone is efficacious: to discover His will and to
do it. This and this alone must govern my actions.

The implications are far-reaching. For after all I have
my own tastes, preferences, pleasures, and sorrows. Life
is made up of sweet and bitter things, stimulating and depressing things. Shall I allow myself to be tossed about by
each passing circumstance? Shall I measure everything
out, choose, vary my pleasures, save a little corner for
inevitable sorrow and suffering, and make a variegated
bouquet to suit my taste? That would amount to practicing
the principle: "I am my own."

But how, then, are we to discern? The will of God mani-
fests itself to us in two general ways: First, through *external Providence,* losses, privations, the demands of our family, of our state of life, of our health. We must recognize
the fatherly will of God in these things. It is something
like the "treasure hidden in a field" of the Gospel. In matters of detail, obedience guides us. If our way of life has
been approved, we have the right to expect in our written
rule, in our living rule, perhaps not the infallible voice of
God but the habitual, providential, reliable and ordinary
help we need to discover and do His will.

Finally, there is *the instinct of the Holy Spirit* who
dwells in us and who leads us through the guidance of our
spiritual director and/or confessor, and through interior
inspirations. Little by little we discern the voice of God,
the good pleasure of God. The rules for the discernment
of spirits help experience, but cannot take its place.

Is everything decided, then? No, not yet. There is
something more than a complicated interplay of mechani-
cal parts between God's will and ours. Our own solution
is correct, elegant, a bit geometrical, somewhat schematic.
Our intellect is satisfied and our will is happy. But there

are also our sensibilities, our imagination, a prism that refracts this light. So many things come between God and me, so many things cut through my life: "Inanimate objects, can it be you have a soul that cleaves to my soul and forces it to love you?"

And if only these things were all inanimate! But they aren't. Some of them are creatures who live, weep, laugh, and bleed with us, tempt us, touch us, importune us, creatures that do us good and evil at one and the same time.

Let us go forward to meet them. Let us question them. Sisters, are you my friends or my enemies? Are you sweet or bitter? Good or evil? The answers are varied. There are mutterings, taunts, calls, songs. Are you creatures of God like me? Here they have to answer "Yes." And if they say they aren't, then they are lying and I shall quickly see it. For the sweat of creatures flows from their every pore.

Well then, let us ply our trade as creatures — you and I. Help me to serve, and I shall help you in my turn. Earth, sea, golden crops, I shall be your voice to praise God our Father. Men, I shall be your helper by my prayers, my actions, my suffering. And you will be my trials, my purification, my patience, my joy, the mirror of my God.

Application of the Fundamental Truths to the Apostolic Life

Man was created. . . . In the case of the apostle we can say that he was created twice. To God's primary intention a second was added: a look of pleasure upon this particular creature, for a specific purpose. And why? In order to fructify within him (and if need be, to endow him with):

1) New aptitudes to make him capable of serving his brothers, of collaborating efficaciously with divine grace, of becoming a "fisher of men." A fisher of men! That is hard. The prey is elusive. The fisherman must go out at night, fight fear, wait, endure the cold, cast his net in vain, and haul it back with difficulty.

2) New desires, a new heart. In place of my small, selfish heart, full of itself, in place of my impure heart, devoid of any real tenderness: "Create a [new] heart in me, O God . . ." (Ps. 50:12). An apostle needs a great heart. God creates such a heart in him.

. . . to praise God, honor Him, serve Him. And to make others praise, honor, and serve Him. The apostle is not supposed to think of himself. "Who is weak, and I am not weak? Who is made to stumble, and I am not inflamed?" (2 Cor. 11:29). So spoke St. Paul. The apostle seeks not his own interests, but "those of Jesus Christ" (Phil. 2:21). He does not seek his own advantage, his own glory, but the advantage and glory of his God.

Everything else must help him in this task. This is another excellent way to discern the will of God among so many creatures jockeying for my attention, my affection, my time. Will my apostolic task be facilitated or hampered by them? Will they make me better able to serve, or will they weigh me down, hold me back, distract me from my goal? Do they diminish my desires, my vocation, my energies for good? Or on the contrary, do they dilate me, and make me more apt and more generous in my work as an apostle?

That is why we must become indifferent (by an effort of the will) to what is pleasant or painful, hard or abhorrent. We must be like soldiers who think only of the task to be done without thought of the danger, of the terrible suffering, of the exhaustion ahead. This attitude can be acquired only by repeated habitual effort, by repeated victories over our own tastes, preferences, and repugnances.

Let us see what our duty demands of us, not simply our duty as creatures but our duty as creatures called to the apostolate. And let us say to God with a new and higher understanding: *I am Thine. I am Thy servant and the son of Thy handmaid, Mary.*

Suggested Reading

Psalms 8, 18, 24, 38, and 39.

The Imitation of Christ, Book III, Chapters 1 and 9; Book II, Chapter 4.

Come, let us glorify the Lord with exultation, . . . let us bend the knees before the Lord who made us. For he is our God; but we are the people of his pasture and the sheep of his hand (Ps. 94:1-7).

Thus saith the Lord thy redeemer,
    the Holy One of Israel:
I am the Lord thy God
    that teach thee profitable things,
    that govern thee in the way that thou walkest.
O that thou hadst hearkened to my commandments!
Thy peace had been as a river,
    and thy justice as the waves of the sea. . . .
His name should not have perished,
    nor have been destroyed from before my face

(Is. 48:17-19).

I am thine (Ps. 118:94).

O Lord, I am thy servant, the son of thy handmaid (Ps. 115:7).

It is not abundance of knowledge that nourishes the soul [spiritually], but savoring things inwardly (St. Ignatius, *Spiritual Exercises,* Annot. 2).

2.

Sin

"Why will you contend with me in judgment? You have all forsaken me, saith the Lord" (Jer. 2:29).

We have all sinned. If our life were spelled out mercilessly before us, with all its weaknesses, base actions, and treacheries, we would hide under the ground.

We have sinned often, seriously, deliberately. For example:

Sentiments of envy, jealousy; thinking with pleasure that we were better than others, preferring ourselves to them; delighting in the evil we heard spoken about others; provoking such evil talk by insincere praise or in some other way.

Officious lies, to excuse ourselves; pretending to know what we did not know out of self-love; exaggerating about ourselves. Citing the words of others in quasi-good faith, coloring them to suit our passions, our own interests, our self-love. False airs of modesty, desires and strategies to be noticed, distinguished, praised, preferred to others; scheming; having to be coaxed; looking for pity.

Taking liberties with words, with our judgments on others; lack of justice, petty calumnies, painting a black picture of our neighbor's actions, interpreting them maliciously, judging them severely, and condemning them rashly; criticizing authority in all its forms. Using words too freely, casting worldly glances, glances of overly natural affection, harsh, complaining, resentful glances, glances of human respect. Vanity, self-love, egoism, stubbornness, pride.

Are we innocent of all these things? If not, we have sinned. And each time we sinned we were saying in effect: "I am my own." We have acted against the fundamental rule. We have acted deliberately, like unjust stewards. For we have received much in the way of light, preservation, and the grace to do the right thing. We have abused many graces. It is a shameful thing to abuse the trust, the kindness of someone. He receives us well, and then we rob him, betray him, tear him to pieces. Well now, were we not well received by our Father in heaven? We have abused His trust, His love. We have offended Him: "I have sinned against thee" (Ps. 40:5). "If I take the wings of the dawn, if I dwell in the uttermost part of the sea: even there will ... thy right hand hold me" (Ps. 138:9-10).

God is the infallible witness who cannot be deceived. "Man seeth those things that appear, but the Lord beholdeth the heart" (1 Kings 16:7). I have often been praised or admired for actions that were mediocre or actually evil.

God is the Just One, the Holy One, who hates sin. Men treat sin as if it were a trifle, and sometimes even praise it. But God judges and punishes sin.

God is Goodness, who deserves to be perfectly loved and served. And what do I amount to? In the eyes of the world? In reality? And I have dared to offend God!

"In the measure that you expiate [your sins] you will know them" (Pascal).

The Sins of the Apostle

All has not been said when we have meditated upon our sins. This is especially true of an apostle whose vocation and grace of state consist in fighting evil in all its forms. We must also meditate upon our sins in terms of their repercussions on others. That is a consideration that should move us deeply.

Our sins diminish and tend to destroy the apostolic efficacy of our efforts. First of all, they dry up the wellsprings of grace that we need to help others and to do our part in saving others. They also combat apostolic zeal within us. For the sinful apostle, striving for goodness becomes a sort of habit, an automatic gesture. There is a flagrant contradiction between his vocation and his state. Little by little this contradiction tends to diminish and then to destroy zeal.

The sins of others also concern the apostle. First, the sins of others that he could prevent but allows to be committed through negligence, laziness, human respect, egoism. On this point we must not get excited and become scrupulous. At the same time, we should not consider sins of omission as vain imaginings.

Moreover — and this is more serious — the apostle may directly encourage and positively occasion the sins of others by his example, particularly in regard to charity or work. What idea of evil, of sin, do we give others? Let us accept the fact that our example will always have a powerful influence on others, either for good or evil. The ideas of those around us with regard to what is good, bad, permissible, forbidden, will depend on what we say no doubt, but also and far more on our habitual way of acting.

Well then, let us ask ourselves what lessons we have given in this matter. Have we given lessons in fervor or indifference? Goodness or evil? Can others conclude when they see us to the dazzling moral superiority of the Catholic faith, to the moral efficacy of our apostolic vocation? What over-all impression do others get of our life?

Our Lord said to His Apostles: "You are the salt of the earth; but if the salt loses its strength, what shall it be salted with? It is no longer of any use but to be thrown out and trodden underfoot by men" (Matt. 5:13). We must be this salt, a principle of purification, of improvement, of savor, a preservative against corruption. But the salt must not lose its strength.

Suggested Reading

The Gospel according to St. Matthew, Chapter 25, Verses 1 to 30.

Psalms 31, 37, 50, and 102.

The Imitation of Christ, Book I, Chapters 21 and 24; Book III, Chapters 50 and 52.

Why will you contend with me in judgment? You have all forsaken me, saith the Lord (Jer. 2:29).

Will a virgin forget her ornament, or a bride her stomacher? But my people hath forgotten me days without number. . . . How exceeding base art thou become, going the same ways over again! (Jer. 2:32, 36).

Yea, I have loved thee with an everlasting love, therefore have I drawn thee, taking pity on thee (Jer. 31:3).

Be astonished, O ye heavens, at this,
    and ye gates thereof, be very desolate, saith the Lord.

For my people have done two evils.
They have forsaken me, the fountain of living water,
And digged to themselves cisterns,
    broken cisterns, that can hold no water

(Jer. 2:12-13).

3.

Note on Lukewarmness and Spiritual Dryness

We must not mistake one for the other. Superficially these two conditions bear a strong resemblance, but basically they are profoundly different.

The lukewarm person is self-satisfied. That is to say, in his relations with God he is without fervor and without fear, without generous love and without any desire for union with Him. He serves God without pushing himself, and that is enough for him. He acts like a well-trained functionary. Above all, no zeal! He has no anxious fear that he may not be doing enough. He is sometimes scrupulous, but never delicate. In his relations with others, he is a bit of a pharisee: "But he spoke this parable also to some who trusted in themselves as being just and despised others" (Luke 18:9). He judges methods, persons, authorities with condescension; he criticizes them, complains about them. He is biased. He almost never accepts reprimands, and never lets anyone guide him. He strives to lead a life in which he will have the maximum of comfort with the minimum of annoyance.

The dry person undergoes a purification of his intellect to strengthen his faith; of his sensibilities to strengthen his generosity and to be made capable of receiving God. Sometimes this experience is both a punishment and a trial, but everyone who expects to lead a serious spiritual life must go through this phase. The dry person passes through more or less prolonged periods of slackness, anxiety, and weariness, "as an arid and parched land, without water" (Ps. 62:3), deprived of the sensible love of his Lord. But deep within him the power that comes from the grace and

love of God continues to act and to function. This power
pulls him away from sin (that is, from consenting to temptation), gives him the instinct to serve others, and to avoid
even slight faults. He is filled with an anxious fear of not
serving God well enough, the desire to please Him, the
yearning to look upon His Face.

Reforming our Will (Matt. 11:25-30)

Three fundamental attitudes are proposed to us in this
text:

1) Evangelical simplicity, founded on humility: "Thou
didst hide these things [mysterious and admirable things
that make Jesus thrill in the Holy Spirit] from the wise
and prudent, and didst reveal them to little ones." Therefore, we must be among these "little ones."

Who are the wise (according to the world)? Those who
are haughty, full of themselves, self-satisfied, proud of their
knowledge, their wisdom, etc.

Who are the prudent (according to the flesh, that is,
according to nature)? Those who are sure of themselves
and of their own ideas, the stubborn, those who are always
"right," who at bottom always want to act only according
to their own prudence.

The "little ones" are not the ignorant, nor the ill-advised,
nor the inexperienced. They are the ones who want only
God, His love, and His service; who do not want to bend
Him to their selfish will, but want to conform their will
to His. They are the ones who know how to see and find
and embrace this truth in providential, human instruments.
Human instruments, and therefore having human faults
and attractions. We must not be discouraged because of
their failings, nor obey them because of their qualities.
Providential instruments, and therefore having the grace
of state. We must see in them the reflection of God's holy
will.

2) "Come to me, all you who labor and are burdened

[with the weight of life, cares, scruples, anxieties, uncertainties]. . . . Take my yoke upon you, and I will give you rest." Come to Me. Therefore, let us seek our strength and our sufficiency not in ourselves, in our will, our temperament, our courage, our unaided efforts, but in our Lord: in prayer and friendly conversation with Him; in Holy Communion and in the Gospels.

3) What are the conditions of this spiritual training and restoration? "Learn from me, for I am meek and humble of heart." To learn of Jesus is to imitate Him:

In meekness. Meekness is more powerful than violence, especially in the spiritual life. Meekness with others and with ourselves. Gentle firmness.

In humility of heart, that is, submission steeped in tenderness, a submission in no sense servile but founded on love. Submission to the providential will of God for us and for those dear to us (in matters of fortune, health, deaths, separations, etc.); submission to God's will of election for us (duties of state, professional obligations, assigned tasks); submission to God's will of attraction and good pleasure, which we are always seeking to discern.

Reforming Our Mind

The reform of our heart and will must be completed by the reform of our mind, which is just as important and as difficult.

To this end we must consider our Lord as our Teacher and picture ourselves sitting at His feet, listening to Him as Mary Magdalene did at Bethany.

He is an original and powerful Teacher, whose teachings are far above any human philosophy. And often without contradicting human wisdom (which also comes from Him), His teachings leave it far behind. Let us consider just a few of His typical lessons, which are particularly appropriate at this moment. They are rules of thinking, of evalua-

tion, whose sometimes paradoxical presentation increases
their incisive power.

"Blessed are they who hunger and thirst for justice,
for they shall be satisfied" (Matt. 5:6). Blessedness (that
is to say, rectitude in one's views and actions) consists
therefore in an eager and pressing desire that the glory
of God may be procured. The essential is this: That "justice" be done; that the kingdom of God come; that His
will be done on earth as it is in heaven; that His name
be hallowed. That is how perfect justice is accomplished.
That is what we must earnestly desire. Hunger, thirst,
these are goads, stimulants to energetic, positive action. A
man who is hungry, and above all a man who is really
thirsty carries everything before him. He is possessed by
his need.

Such must be our rule of thinking. All of the rest, important as it may seem, is trifling compared to the price
of this justice. The kingdom of God! That is the primary,
the fundamental point. Those who hunger and thirst for
it will be "satisfied" on the last day when all justice will
be done. But even in this life they will know that the
only-begotten Son, our Lord Jesus Christ, has already
given all glory to God.

"Blessed are the clean of heart, for they shall see God"
(Matt. 5:8). This beatitude consists in innocence of life,
whether preserved or regained, in the simplicity of an up-
right, innocent soul that wills what is good. A soul so
blessed has no secret intentions, is not crafty, deceitful, or
full of intrigue and selfish tactics. In its absence of malice,
it is the soul of a child.

These are the souls that "shall see God." God's action
in the world of souls and in history is like His action on
the physical world. It is so far-reaching and goes so deep
that a superficial observer may fail to discern it. Here
again, God does not take the place of, does not annihilate
secondary causes. He uses them. And it follows that we

can always find a natural explanation for everything. It is not a sufficient and ultimate reason, but it is compelling enough to give us the illusion that it explains everything.

Gross, carnal souls, attached to the senses, contracted by egoism, blinded by pride, do not see through appearances and secondary causes. They do not see God. They are too imperfect as mirrors to reflect the august simplicity of God's action. The heart that is darkened, infatuated by the vapors of self-love and sensuality, is too imperfect to sense this action, too different from it to resound in unison with it.

Only the pure heart sees through appearances, goes beyond secondary causes, and without misjudging or ignoring intermediate actions, finds its God in all things. It is neither scandalized nor disturbed by the unfathomable, inscrutable, incomprehensible ways of Providence. Its faith and trust remain unshaken amid the most terrible temptations.

This intimate view of divine action, this habitual way of thinking, acting, and living in the presence of God is the joy of the saints upon earth, and the source of their fruitfulness.

Suggested Reading

The Gospel according to St. Luke, Chapter 15.

Psalms 41, 54, and 117.

The Imitation of Christ, Book I, Chapter 25; Book III, Chapter 52.

Wherefore I say to thee, her sins, many as they are, shall be forgiven her, because she has loved much (Luke 7:47).

And when [Martha] had said this, she went away and quietly called Mary her sister, saying, "The Master is here and calls thee" (John 11:28).

4.

Note on Compunction

The compunction to which the gift of tears is akin is not the selfish, carnal, "Babylonian" sadness that we cannot make ourselves admit. Nor is it the superficial ennui of self-love, cowardice, sloth, boredom. And yet there is a certain ennui that comes close to compunction. This is the sacred ennui that sleeps in all profound hearts, the consuming desire for God: "For to me to live is Christ, and to die is gain" (1 Phil. 1:21). Nor is it to be confused with the melancholy, affected gloom, and spiritual vacuousness that are sources of moral debility.

Compunction comes *from above,* and consists in experiencing the personal misery shared by all men in this valley of tears. We sense we are sinful and weak, and become aware of our tendencies to evil.

The priest expresses these sentiments at the Offertory of the Mass: "pro innumerabilibus peccatis, et offensionibus, et negligentiis meis — for mine own countless sins, offenses, and negligences. . . ."

Compunction does not destroy our courage or even our cheerfulness. But through it we say: "Have mercy on me, Lord, for I know my wickedness."

The Presentation of Jesus in the Temple

Let us contemplate Jesus as Mary offered Him up to God His Father.

What do we mean by "contemplate"? An excellent and very sweet way of praying. There are some who can almost never "meditate," that is, follow an orderly train of thought on a spiritual subject, pausing at ideas that stir them, and then drawing conclusions. Others who are usually able to meditate are sometimes tired of doing it, exhausted, eager to find something simpler. Then contemplation presents itself as a possibility.

Contemplation consists in rendering a mystery present to our minds by sight, sound, touch, by all the spiritual senses. Here again there is a great diversity of attractions and aptitudes. Some are auditory, others visual, or even muscular. There are those who see things in detail, and others who see them as a whole. But whatever our method, we render the mystery present to ourselves. And we let this sight, these words, these examples produce their natural and supernatural fruit within us. We let our paltry fruit ripen within us under the sun.

The activity involved on our part may vary greatly. Some use all their ingenuity to picture themselves as paupers, unworthy servants, wrapping the Child Jesus in His swaddling clothes and preparing His manger. Others remain there, quietly attentive to the mystery of the Cross, letting Jesus' words from the Cross fall straight down upon their soul and into their heart. It is a good thing to ask for spiritual favors in the beginning, but after that we should let things take their course.

What is the subject of our contemplation here? Mary and Joseph come to the Temple to offer up the Child: a tiny baby, all wrapped in white, barely two months old. He does not talk, He does not cry. He is in His mother's arms.

St. Joseph carries two turtledoves in a little basket.

Mary, after she has presented herself to the high priest as the Law requires and has fulfilled the rites, offers her Son to God His Father, as does the priest at the Elevation of the Mass.

Mary is there, and this is her only Son, living, breathing.

She knows she is offering up a Victim.

She knows for whom she is offering Him. She foresees all the future ingratitudes, and the faithful who are to come.

She knows why she is offering Him, and to what a fate! She has read Isaias 53.

She knows the ransom for which she is offering Him — the remission of our sins.

Now come Simeon and Anna the prophetess. They praise God.

Let us listen to the *Nunc Dimittis:* ". . . because my eyes have seen thy salvation, which thou hast prepared before the face of all peoples: a light of revelation to the Gentiles . . ." (Luke 2:30-32). It is an *apostolic canticle.*

"A sign that shall be contradicted" (Luke 2:34).

"And thy own soul a sword shall pierce" (Luke 2:35).

Suggested Reading

Psalms 72, 76, 120, 122, 124, 126.

The Imitation of Christ, Book III, Chapters 27, 32, and 37.

I praise thee, Father, Lord of heaven and earth, that thou didst hide these things from the wise and prudent, and didst reveal them to little ones (Matt. 11:25).

Take this short and perfect word: Forsake all and thou shalt find all, leave thy desires and thou shalt find rest. . . .

Lord, this is no one-day's work, no child's play; yea, in this short sentence is included the whole perfection of a religious man.

Son, thou must not be turned back, nor presently cast down, when thou hearest what the way of the perfect is: but rather be incited thereby to undertake great things, or at least to sigh after them with an earnest desire (*Imitation,* Book III, Chapter 32, 1-3).

V

THE MEANING OF LIFE

1.

The Meaning of Our Life

Let us meditate on the basic principles of the *Spiritual Exercises*. But before presenting a few considerations on this subject, I must tell you the dispositions you should have to make the *Exercises* well. Chief among them are: 1) Interior peace, and avoidance of agitation. As the result of fatigue or inexperience, we may be very dry. The essential is not to have beautiful thoughts or even great desires, but "to savor things inwardly." The taste may not be delicious. It need only be substantial. When war rations are well assimilated they provide excellent nourishment. 2) Trust in God, and a firm resolve to serve Him alone at our own expense, at all costs. Moreover these dispositions are independent of the sweetness that God sometimes gives us, and distinct from natural fervor. Soldiers lacking "enthusiasm" are sometimes the best, providing the sacred fire of patriotism burns deep within them.

Man was created to praise God, to honor and serve Him. . . .

These very simple words open the portion of the *Exercises* that we are about to meditate upon. This fundamental

65

truth can be presented under many aspects. St. Paul used to say: *"You are not your own"* (1 Cor. 6:19): Your life does not belong to you, it is not a resource, a good that you may exploit as you please, to your own advantage, according to your own whims. In the parable of the talents Our Lord expresses the same doctrine: our powers to love, to understand, to feel, are not possessions which we, as owners, may use and abuse. They are gifts, loans, for which we shall have to give an account. We are responsible for them. St. Ignatius recalls that it is the power of God, His goodness, His infinite wisdom that has called us into being. Of ourselves we could not give ourselves life. We are not *necessary* beings, *eternal* beings. We have received from God life, grace, all that we have and all that we are.

It follows, therefore, that we belong to Him. We owe to Him all that we have received. We owe ourselves to Him. Hence it is an absolute misconception to say: "I will live my own life, I owe no one any accounting." It is also an injustice, a theft. We appropriate what is not ours. Thus it is an inconsistency, an error, a sin, to acknowledge our dependence in principle while taking back and appropriating our life in its particulars. Our only true purpose is to return our life to God, to use it according to His known will. It is wisdom now, and it will be our happiness later. Every instrument rightly used for its true purpose performs good work. When we accept and seek God's will, we cannot fail to attain our last end.

Thus everything converges to make us praise, love, and serve God: loyalty, integrity, a correct understanding of our own interest. The gift of our life to God has two elements: the first is affective, the second is effective and practical.

The affective element consists of a threefold homage:

1) Homage of the mind by which we acknowledge our total dependence: "Thou art my God." "O Lord, I am thy servant, the son of thy handmaid" (Ps. 115:7). "Thy hands have made me and formed me" (Ps. 118:73). "I am thine."

2) Homage of words, by which we proclaim this dependence outwardly: "I praise thee, Father, Lord of heaven and earth . . ." (Matt. 11:25). "Our Father who art in heaven, hallowed be thy name. . . ." "I am thine."

3) Homage of the heart, by which we delight in this absolute dependence: "Yes, Father, for such was thy good pleasure" (Matt. 11:26). "I am thine."

The effective element consists in action which corresponds to our threefold homage, that is, in the service of God. This service has three principal marks:

1) It is *unlimited*. It is not a bilateral contract, a hiring out of a part of our activity. We have sold the tree with the fruit, the vine arbor with the grapes.

2) It is *unconditional,* because God alone is the Master. He alone is all just and all good. His will is good, totally good. Let us try to savor His infinite goodness.

3) It is *filial,* because it is not addressed to a Law, a Fatality, but to a Love (God is Love), to a Father, our Father: "audemus dicere: Pater noster — we make bold to say: Our Father. . . ."

Mary's words say everything: "Behold the handmaid of the Lord."

The Use of Creatures

The purpose of life, of all human life, of our own individual life, is to praise and serve God. In a word, it is to render to God the things that are God's. The fulfillment of this duty coincides with the First Commandment. For it is essentially directed to making us love God with our whole heart, with our whole mind, and with all our strength. It assures the attainment of our last end, for it establishes us firmly in a climate of everyday reality.

But — and there is always a "but" — in practice, the homage and service we owe to God run afoul of difficulties from the outside and encounter inward obstacles on our part. Actually we have simplified the problem by reducing it to a dialogue between God our Creator, Master, and Father, and ourselves. There is more to consider.

There are the material helps which sustain our life; for it is a paltry little flame. It needs oil to feed it. We need clothing, food, a bed to rest on. There are spiritual elements which we cannot do without, and which come to us from other human creatures: the knowledge we borrow or obtain from others; affection, our life of human relations, friendship, business, and conversation of all sorts.

And in this motley world, our great fundamental obligation finds both allies and enemies. Among our allies: the mother who teaches us to praise God, the teacher who teaches us to know Him, the priest who shows us the efficacious ways of serving Him, the friend who encourages us to do good or brings us back to it, the good book, the good organization, the good work. And the enemies: the companion who teaches us evil, the teacher of error, the unfaithful friend, the bad book, the evil pleasure, the wicked man.

To maintain our course amid these conflicting forces, what do we need? In the measure that we become more autonomous, that we let go of our mother's hand, we need a luminous rule, an education, a practical, effective spiritual formation.

The luminous rule is easy to formulate: I must treat creatures as means. For all these creatures between God and me, that I need and that often need me, are means and not ends in themselves; they must help me to attain my essential end and not divert me from it. Now a means is strictly subordinate to the end. When we are trying to get out of a ditch, we do not look to see if someone is holding out to us a cane with an ivory head or a rough and thorny cudgel. When we are rushing to the side of a loved one who is dying, any vehicle will do providing it takes us to our destination.

In short, we pay little attention to the accidental aspects of a means. We make use of it or refrain from using it in the measure that it serves our purpose. We would refuse a superb limousine that could not maneuver a narrow country road in favor of an outmoded and uncomfortable cart. What we want is to reach our destination. Let us apply this to creatures: I must make use of them in the measure that they help me to serve God, to praise Him, whether they are attractive or irksome. I must keep away from them, ignore them, even despise them in the full measure that they would keep me from serving and praising Him. That is the rule.

It is all very clear, but impossible to observe in practice unless we have had effective training in the habit of bridling our antipathies and blunting our attraction for created things. This rule is like a winter sun: it illumines the last fruits of the season but does not ripen them. Why? Because we are not simply rational animals, we are also animals with emotions. And often we are more emotional than rational. Then attractions and aversions have a powerful effect on us, as experience well shows.

What practical, effective training will enable us to habitually observe the rule upon which rests the fulfillment of our fundamental and primary duty as creatures of God? A deliberate formation of renunciation with reference to certain attractions, and of courage in the face of certain aversions.

The word "certain" as used here means something special, something different for each of us. For one, it is the attraction of satisfied vanity, of sensuality, of sloth, of wanting to have our own way and to make our ideas prevail, of passionate and jealous friendships, etc. For another, it is repugnance in the face of apostolic effort, aversion to peaceful, steadfast hope, to trust, and so on.

In addition to the negative aspect of this training, with its emphasis on abnegation and mortification, there is a positive aspect that consists in developing within us through meditation, prayer, desire, and inclination, a taste for the will of God, a love for His infinite Goodness. Then, regardless of its disguise, we shall love it and delight in it. But first we shall find it, we shall sense it, just as St. Francis Borgia instinctively sensed the real presence of Christ, just as St. John sensed that his beloved Master was there. *Lord, I have found You!*

Note on Three Ways of Meditating Simply

1) Choosing a phrase that we savor and allow to be diffused like a piece of candy within us: "The Master is here and calls thee" (John 11:28). "Behold the handmaid of the Lord" (Luke 1:38).

2) A simple glance, whether general or detailed, upon the exterior of a mystery, savoring the inward reality expressed by the whole or by one of its details.

3) Our simple, attentive, loving presence.

Suggested Reading

Psalms 23, 24, 25, and 91.

The Imitation of Christ, Book III, Chapters 1, 2, 9, and 10.

Behold the handmaid of the Lord (Luke 1:38).

It is good for me to be near to God, to put my trust in the Lord God (Ps. 72:28).

[Lord], make known to me the way I should walk because to thee I lift up my soul. . . . Teach me to do thy will, because thou art my God. Thy spirit is good: may it lead me to a land that is smooth (Ps. 142:8, 10).

Speak, speak, Lord, Thy servant hears.
I say: Thy servant, for that is what I am.
I am Thy servant, and such I want to be, to walk along
    Thy path both day and night
        (*Imitation,* Book III, Chapter 2, translated by Pierre
        Corneille).
Lord, I have found You . . .

                      (Paul Claudel, *Magnificat*).

2.

The Parable of the Talents

In the parables we must distinguish the principal lesson from the moral of the fable, laying stress on the former and using the latter only to the extent that it serves to fix our attention. In this parable, the lesson is very clear. It concerns the obligations incumbent upon us as the result of God's gifts, of all God's gifts to us.

1) The talents God gives are very different, very unequal. The word *talent* signifies in its origins a sum, a weight of money. In the parable the talents refer to a sum to be used to advantage, taken as the symbol of all talent in the current sense of the word. Are we grateful to God for the talents that we have received?

2) God proportions His gifts to the capacities of each one: "to each according to his particular capacity" (Matt. 25:15). And He leaves a great deal to our own personal initiative: "and then he went on his journey" (*ibid.*). Evidently divine grace is always with us, but in the last analysis our collaboration is indispensable.

3) Five talents, two talents, one talent. Let those who have, or think they have received less take care lest they depend too much on the others. In the parable it is the servant who received the least who was the most unfaithful.

4) Giving an account. We have to do it sooner or later. And we must give an account of *all* the talents we have received. He who has received five and gained five more has used his talents to the fullest advantage. He is fully rewarded: "Well done, good and faithful servant . . . enter into the joy of thy master" (Matt. 25:21). You have followed your motto, "I will serve!" Everything in you has served well: your mind, your heart, your powers of soul and body. So too with the one who received two talents. The same fidelity, although his starting point and the plentitude of his gifts were very different. And he too receives the same reward.

5) The unfaithful servant. He knew and even greatly exaggerated the demands of his master. It was probably his excessive and harmful apprehension, his sinful lack of trust that led him to inertia, laziness, failure. Let him not say: "I could not do it!" For he, like the others, received according to his capacities. Let him not say: 'Too much was demanded of me!" For all that was asked of him was that he fructify one talent. He is unforgivable.

I shall ask our Lord for the trust and courage necessary to turn all my talents to account, including my talent for the apostolate. *I will serve!*

Compunction

We are determined, with the grace of God, to sincerely seek and generously accomplish the will of God. But the evangelical saying remains: "Blessed are the clean of heart, for they shall see God" (Matt. 5:8).

The judgment is this: The Light came into the world, and men preferred darkness to the light, for their works were evil. For he who does evil hates the light and does not come to the light, for fear that his works will be condemned. But he who acts righteously comes to the light, so that the beauty of his actions may be made manifest (Cf. John 1:1-18).

It follows that whoever wants to know the will of God habitually and fulfill it faithfully must be pure. He must either remain pure or become pure again. Purification of soul is of the highest importance, and although it may have painful aspects, we must meditate on it in calm fervor, in peaceful compunction.

Compunction is the fundamental sentiment that must dominate, because no other sentiment is more effective in deepening within us the horror, the fear, and the hatred of evil. Compunction is a metaphorical expression like contrition. Whereas contrition bespeaks a bruising, breaking, and crushing, compunction is a transfixion, a transverberation, a piercing blow like the one the aged Simeon spoke of: "And thy own soul a sword shall pierce."

When compunction has become habitual, it is the attitude of someone who has received this blow, who knows what is in man and in himself in the way of misery, weakness, attachment to evil, complicity, and complacency. Such a man is therefore in a state of humble mistrust of himself, of scorn for himself, and of constant appeal to God. Compunction, therefore, is not sadness born of one's temperament, or of external accident, or of self-love. It is not melancholy, a vague spiritual malaise, the odious romantic debility which is the enemy of virile action. On the contrary, compunction is perfectly at home with cheerfulness, peace, and spiritual joy. It is their older sister, the one who maintains and feeds the family. St. Thérèse of the Child Jesus, after her transverberation, was a living embodiment, a powerhouse of spiritual and familial joy.

Compunction, the daughter of God, is the truth about ourselves and about the world of humanity. It is the prerequisite of humility, innocence, and serious, efficacious love. And the truth that frees us from our illusions, our presumptions, our ignorance, our selfish weaknesses is this: We are members of a sinful race, deserving only punishment and scorn. We belong to a vile and evil throng. We are bound up with them, we are an integral part of the whole. So we have no cause to be proud, to remain aloof, and to say: "We are not like the rest of men" (cf. Luke 18:11). There are many who deceive themselves on this score.

How can we tell that this is so? By reason of the fact that quite apart from our more or less serious sins, we have within us inclinations, predispositions to every evil. Within us are the roots of sin, of all sin. Every manner of evil finds us willing accomplices. Our faculties for the most part are darkened, sullied, deflected toward evil.

Our intellect: frivolous, incapable of sustained effort,

with a tendency to judge quickly, harshly, unfairly, in the worst possible light; superficial, narrow, seduced by appearances, enigmatic, a mystery to ourselves.

Our will: weak, acting by fits and starts, feeble and brittle, docile to evil influences, almost impervious to good ones; inclined to dissipation, vain; headstrong, stubborn as a mule in the face of trifling obstacles in wounded sensibilities.

Our sensibilities: cold and devoid of generosity toward God; demanding and passionate where we are concerned; expecting much and giving little; jealous, tyrannical, absorbing; excessive in their manifestations, or haughty and distant; indiscreet in their demands, uncontrolled like those of a spoiled child.

Our imagination: quick to review and brood over anything that arouses our anger, indignation, resentment, melancholy, and willful sadness; wandering with pleasure around the edges of forbidden pits of corruption and sin; exaggerating everything, making the world we live in one of fantasy and unreality.

Our body: temperament and health subject to every ill; frail, easily exhausted, out of kilter, agitated, incapable of regular, prolonged work.

All these things make up man as he is. These are the things that I am made of. And from this must come a refined instrument, a chosen arrow, a vessel of honor, an apostle: "this man is a chosen vessel to me" (Acts 9:15). From this chaos, a masterpiece must come forth. How? God knows, and He will accomplish it if we are faithful. There are Jesus, Mary, the Cross, Holy Communion, the Gospel, the saints, obedience, fraternal charity. We have all the balms and remedies we need. But the condition for using them is to know what we are, so that we may become pure. We must realize that we are sinners, the sons of sinners.

The Inevitable Penance

We have meditated on the roots of sin within us. But these roots have put forth countless poisonous shoots and fruits of death. It is not enough for us to say: "In sin did my mother conceive me" (Ps. 50:7). (In short, I belong to a sinful race.) We must also say: "Against thee have I sinned and, what is evil in thy sight, I have done" (Ps. 50:6).

All our real sins, that is, those for which we are personally responsible, stem from our immoderate love of self. I owe my whole being to God. To sin is to withdraw from His control, to set myself up temporarily as my own last end, to prefer myself to Him.

This egoistical, evil "self," consists first of all in my proud, self-sufficient, vain, haughty self. It is the source of all my desires to make a good appearance, to excel, to be listened to, and to have my opinions prevail not because they are good but because they are mine. It is the instigator of all my efforts to set myself off, to distinguish myself, to be loved, preferred. And the tactics it suggests include false modesty, timidity, exaggerations, lies, boasting, trifling excuses; harshness, injustice, slander, malicious reports, jealousy, partiality, unfair judgments. Not to mention stubborness, impatience, resentment, willful sadness, tears of self-pity. And of course self-satisfaction, excessive love of my own independence, of my freedom of action, suspicion, and presumption.

Then there is my sensual, nonchalant, pleasure-seeking self. This is the source of my negligence, gluttony, sloth, laxity, and immodesty. As also of the liberties I take in the books I read, the plays I see, my conversations, my daydreams, my imaginary or real affections, that are too keenly felt, too exclusive, too exciting. And of course of my omissions, my indifference, my human respect, my resistance to grace, my fears of doing the right thing, the better thing.

All these sins have a very ugly common denominator: they spell out the fact that we are sinners, that we have sinned deliberately, like unjust stewards. We have sinned after receiving so many favors from God, so many graces of attraction, preservation, and light. We have abused God's mercy. It is shameful to abuse our parents' trust: "Son, everything I have is yours. Here are my keys. You are in your own home!" And then the son takes everything, diverts it to his own profit, squanders it. He goes even further. He brings his debauched friends into his father's house, mocks his father, insults him, tears him apart with words. He abuses him.

We have committed these sins before the face of God: "Against thee have I sinned and, what is evil in thy sight, I have done" (Ps. 50:6). "Man seeth those things that appear, but the Lord beholdeth the heart" (1 Kings 16:7). God is the infallible witness. He said to me: "Walk before me and be perfect" (Gen. 17:1). And I answered: "I shall walk before thee and I shall be a sinner!"

God is the Just One, the Holy One. I have treated as a trifle or as a cumbersome scruple what He judges to be evil and wrong.

Note on Corporeal Penance

A few words on penance, notably corporeal penance.

In principle, we recognize and profess the importance, indeed the necessity of corporeal penance. First because it is a guarantee of the sincerity of our interior religion. (If we accept difficult and painful things for the sake of someone, it is a proof of our love for him.) Second, because it is an indispensable means of keeping ourselves spiritually in form. Indifference, laxity, weakness of will, excessive sensitiveness — in short *fear of blows* — constitute basic obstacles to the devout, perfect, and apostolic life. Penance is a necessary limbering-up exercise, an exercise of spiritual training, of ascesis. Third, because penance satisfies our conscious need of reparation, our just anger against ourselves. When we acknowledge that we have been weak, evil, and unworthy, we are filled with holy indignation and we want to avenge outraged justice on ourselves.

Fourth, penance is necessary and important because Jesus suffered in His flesh and we want to configure ourselves to Him. "With Christ I am nailed to the cross" (Gal. 2:19). All the saints have been penitents. And so even if we cannot practice penance, we must praise it, desire it, and love it.

In practice, we often remain novices in this matter, very far removed from the red roses of Carmel. And the reason for this may be twofold: on the one hand, the burden of excessive work, or at least of tasks that are habitually very absorbing; and on the other hand a correlative lack of robust health. But even though the penance we can actually practice is very slight in view of the frailty of our health and the burden of work, we must still practice it. It is an indispensable sign of fervor.

Suggested Reading

Penitential Psalms 5, 31, 37, 50, 101, 129, and 142.

The Imitation of Christ, Book I, Chapters 21, 22, and 23.

There is no health in my flesh because of thy indignation, there is no soundness in my bones on account of my sin (Ps. 37:4).

> What shall I, frail man, be pleading,
> Who for me be interceding,
> When the just are mercy needing?
>
> (Sequence: *Dies Irae*).

Lord Jesus Christ, Thou didst say by the mouth of the Prophet "with an everlasting love, I have mercifully drawn thee to myself," wherefore I beseech Thee that Thou wouldst deign to offer and present unto God the Father almighty that same love which brought Thee down to earth from heaven in order

to endure all Thy bitter suffering. May God accept Thy offering on behalf of the soul of this Thy servant, and may He
deliver him from the punishment and suffering he fears in
retribution for his sins . . .

(*Roman Ritual,* Commending the Departing Soul to God).

3.

On the Parables of Mercy (Luke 15:1-10)

We might well meditate upon the beautiful parable of
the Prodigal Son, but we prefer to pause at the two little
parables that precede it. Here the role of the sinner is not
spelled out in detail as in the Prodigal Son, nor is the sinner's responsibility stressed as in the parable of the Talents.
No, the sinner is represented as a wanderer, a lost sheep,
a lost drachma. No one says: "It is his fault." But we
know very well, in our own case, where the fault lies. What
these two little parables bring out with piercing clarity is
the infinite mercy of Our Lord that never grows weary.

He is the Good Shepherd. Here is His flock: a hundred
sheep that He is leading to pasture. He watches over them,
not with an over-all impersonal glance, but sees each one
individually. It is men who take a general view of things.
God sees and loves distinctly, personally. The Good Shepherd knows His sheep, and they know Him: "He calls his
own sheep by name" (John 10:3). He knows them and
calls each one, and each one knows Him, knows who He is.

The Shepherd loses one of them. "What man of you
having a hundred sheep, and losing one of them. . . ." What
delicacy! It seems as if it were just an accident. It is
nobody's fault, or rather it is the Shepherd who blames
Himself: "I have lost one of My sheep."

What is He going to do? Turn His attention to the
others? After all, He still has ninety-nine, practically all
of them. The one who got lost is simply an unfortunate
stray, "the child of perdition" that is never lacking. Or
will the Good Shepherd, moved to pity, seek out the lost

one? And then, will He send someone to find it, one of
His youthful helpers? That would already be very good.
But no, that is not enough. No doubt this servant would
treat the poor wanderer brutally. And besides, would he
find it? Would he look for it the way he should? No, the
Shepherd will go *Himself*. He will leave His faithful flock
behind. He will return to the thorny thickets over there,
where He thinks the poor little one is.

And when He has found it! Instead of meting out stern
punishment to it as it deserves, "he lays it upon his shoulders rejoicing" (Luke 15:5). And He calls together His
friends, the Saints and the Angels, and the Blessed Virgin,
to rejoice with Him.

> *O Jesu, Bone Pastor, Panis vere,*
> *Jesu, nostri miserere. . . .*

Trust, love.

The Apostolic Call

Once our life has been ordered to God and returned to
Him (at least in principle) as its sole legitimate Master,
and once it has been purified by compunction and repentance for our sins, we must consecrate it to the service of
our Lord. That is an indispensable turning point. Up to
that time, we have conducted ourselves the way every good
Christian can and must if he wants to be faithful to grace.

From then on the apostolic call can and in fact is heard
by those who will follow: "Come, follow me, and I will
make you fishers of men" (Matt. 4:19). In other words,
come, follow my example. I will take persons who were
merely seeking an honest livelihood (by casting their nets),
or a means of winning power, or an opportunity for intellectual development, or perhaps all of these things at once
— which is very praiseworthy — and I will make *apostles*
of them.

Come, follow Me, learn of Me. This is an invitation that
all Christians understand and must accept. But "I will

make you fishers of men" is something else again. No
doubt every faithful disciple is already an apostle. By virtue of the communion of saints, every good thing he does
benefits his brothers. By virtue of fraternal charity and
example, he strives to do good and succeeds. But he has
not yet been chosen, set apart, and exclusively dedicated
to the work of God, as were Peter and Andrew, Paul and
Barnabas, Ignatius and Xavier. Some of us have summed
up this vocation, discerned and followed it, accepted and
lived it, in a vow consecrating our life to the work of God.

We must hear this call and make it more distinct, or
resurrect it within us with all its practical consequences,
with all its divine power. For this vocation effects what
it signifies: it presupposes aptitudes, but it also stirs up
within us appropriate energies, graces, capacities for doing
the good thing, the better thing. "You have not chosen me,
but I have chosen you, and have appointed you that you
should go and bear fruit, and that your fruit should remain"
(John 15:16). Let us meditate upon these words.

Come, follow Me. Come with Me. It is an invitation,
more or less imperative, but never a strict command. To
the rich young man Jesus said: "If thou wilt be perfect
. . . come, follow me." If thou wilt. . . .

Jesus teaches a fundamental lesson that every good
Christian must learn. But there is another lesson which
demands separation from the rest, exile. It is a lesson
meant for those who want to distinguish themselves, sacrifice themselves, give themselves, but first and above all
who want to be with Him. He is the nerve-center, the bond
of all things.

Therefore, I call upon you to follow Christ more closely,
very closely, as closely as possible, your steps in His. Accept and love, profess and carry out not only His positive
commands but also His counsels; not only His general
wishes, but His special preferences. At this price you will
become His companion, His servant, His "man," His crea-

ture, His *alter ego,* His apostle. At this price you will become His representative, His intimate and constant collaborator (not a temporary and accidental one) in spreading the kingdom of God upon earth. At this price, you will become His friend, His disciple, His betrothed, and in a real sense His spouse.

"I will make you fishers of men." How? Here St. Ignatius (whose spirit we are faithfully following) stops and says: "Attention! Do not work yourself up. Do not confuse the call of God with human enthusiasm, the true gift of self with phantasy, illusion! The teaching of Jesus is not what a frivolous world thinks it is. You must take a frank, dispassionate view of His counsels, His tastes, His preferences, for you will be expected to love, savor, and practice them. You must even pursue this inquiry with a rigor that will safeguard you against any subsequent surprise attack." You must see things in their worst (or is it their best?) light. The preferences, the counsels of Jesus are these: *abnegation, renunciation,* notably in three areas:

1) The area of ease, comfort, sensible pleasure, well-being, work freely chosen. An apostle must know how to do without these things. He must know how to make use of them, but to this end he must first do without them, lead a hard, rugged life, deprived of many of the pleasures others enjoy. Anyone who does not agree to this condition is simply a dreamer of heroic dreams.

2) The area of our sensibilities and sensible affections. We cannot choose our companions. A certain austerity is indispensable. Certain affections must be denied. All the other affections, even the most legitimate and necessary, must be purified, spiritualized, and hence mortified, emancipated from immediate self-interested pleasure. "Whom have I in Heaven but thee? And if I am with thee, earth does not delight me" (Ps. 72:25).

Even the spiritual delights of solitary prayer and of the prayer of union will have to be subordinated to our apostolic work.

3) The area of manifested esteem. Not only must vanity, lies, false pretense, worldliness in the strict sense be mortified, combatted, gradually eliminated. Even our concern about our reputation, about what people think or say of us will have to be mortified by submission, obedience, self-effacement, painful effort, total disinterestedness in promoting the good of our common undertaking.

These are the conditions of our apostolic engagement. "Are you willing?"

The Apostolic Call of Jesus

Now that we have considered the apostolic call and the conditions of this call, let us meditate upon the apostolic call that Jesus received, and its conditions.

We shall picture the Blessed Virgin in her oratory, that is, in a quiet room of her parents' house. She prays as she works with her hands, as she spins. She prays, and naturally her prayer takes the form of a powerful imploration and finds expression in words of Scripture: "Come Lord, do not delay!" "Drop down dew, ye heavens, from above, and let the clouds rain the just!" (Is. 45:8). She prays, and through her pure lips, through her innocent soul, through her spirit in which the Spirit of God reigns and groans ineffably, it is the whole human race, it is you and I who implore, who pray.

Look down, Lord, and see. See into what state your chosen vine, the house of Israel has fallen. Pharisaism constricts and sterilizes, hardens and poisons even the most zealous. As for the others, they drink in iniquity like water. And the rest of the world "sits in darkness and in the shadow of death" (cf. Ps. 106:10). Profound darkness. True, there is a Roman power, the *Pax Romana*. True, there is Greek art as well as Greek literature. But none of these have the power to redeem, to purify, to illumine. "To the Unknown God!" (Acts 17:23). This is the cry that Paul would later repeat: to the true God, the God who is greater than dead gods, to the living and seeing God, to the One who was, is, and will be.

Throughout the world, what sinfulness, what misery! The Herods, the princes and the powerful men, the little folk, the slaves. St. Paul describes it all to us in his Epistle to the Romans (1:24-32). We can hardly bare to read it. And John speaks of it in the eighteenth chapter of his Apocalypse.

There still remains good will, souls inwardly orientated toward Christianity, traces of light, appeals to the dimly glimpsed Good, the Liberator, the Master who teaches the ways of the Lord in truth, the Redeemer who purifies. They are like those spirits Vergil talks about, seeking peace amid their harassment and wanderings: "They held out their hands with love to the other shore. . . ."[1]

Father Martindale tells us: "Plato was already saying that wretched humanity had only one thing to do, namely, to cast itself into the troubled water of life, clinging to everything it might find at hand in the way of hopes, conjectures, myths, and rites, until the day it could reach the other shore on the more trustworthy ship of a few divine doctrines."[2]

Such is humanity's cry. We belong to the human race, and we too cry out: "Come, Lord Jesus!" Without you, what a void, what helplessness, what uncertainty! What frightful chaos, what unforgivable sins, what gross, empty, and shameful pleasures!

But how this cry gains in efficacy in passing through the most pure lips of Mary. She alone is untainted by original corruption, she alone is immaculate, perfectly chaste, redeemed beforehand and perfectly pleasing. The Word of God hears her cry and agrees to come.

But Lord, before you accept your apostolic call, consider

---

[1] *Aeneid,* Book VI, v. 314.
[2] *Christus,* 1913 edition, p. 405.

the conditions of your coming. We invoke you, we implore you, yes. But if you come, if you take on a human nature to redeem us (not from above, the way a rich man buys a flock of sheep or the way the masters of antiquity bought an army of slaves), if you come in peace, fraternally, the way an older brother redeems his younger brothers, the way a father redeems his sons, then you will become as one of us!

In all things except sin. It goes without saying that moral evil is incompatible with divine purity. But you will share in everything else. You will have a mind like ours that does not grasp everything at a single glance, a heart that can suffer and be wounded by ingratitude and crudeness; you will have sensibilities, and flesh that can be bruised, torn. Yes, you will have all these human attributes. To this point you will humble yourself. You will be the *Son of man,* born of woman. You will be the tiny, fragile, trembling, wailing thing that is a baby. You will weep, you will be hungry, you will grow tired.

People will be unkind to you, they will misjudge you, they will be unable to recognize your love. And *I* shall be ungrateful!

They will beat you, make a laughing stock of you, scourge you. They will deny you, be ashamed of you. And *I* shall be ashamed of you!

They will forget you, they will prefer Barabbas and so many others to you. They will even prefer before you abstractions like the "Humanity" you are going to redeem. They will prefer idols of flesh, painted, empty idols, demons of pride, tyrants "who kill the body" (Luke 12:4). And *I* shall prefer my own pleasure to you! "Depart from me, Lord!"

The Word was made flesh, and dwelt among us. He becomes incarnate within Mary, full of grace and truth. He chooses Apostles, trains them, sends them forth, makes their words efficacious. At our birth He marks us with His sign.

With wonderful providence He directs all events. He invites us to follow Him: "If you want to follow Me. . . ."

Yes, Lord. Your country will be my country. Your tastes, my tastes. *With you.* . . .

Suggested Reading

Psalms 62, 64, 71, and 72.

The Imitation of Christ, Book II, Chapter 7; Book III, Chapter 5.

And he said to them, "Come, follow me, and I will make you fishers of men." And at once they left [their father and] their nets, and followed him (Matt. 4:19-20).

The young man said to him, "All these I have kept; what is yet wanting to me?" Jesus said to him, "If thou wilt be perfect, go, sell what thou hast, and give to the poor . . . . and come, follow me." But when the young man heard the saying, he went away sad, for he had great possessions (Matt. 19:20-22).

From that time Jesus began to show his disciples that he must go to Jerusalem and suffer many things . . . and be put to death . . . . And Peter taking him aside, began to chide him, saying, "Far be it from thee, O Lord; this will never happen to thee." He turned and said to Peter, "Get behind me, satan, thou art a scandal to me; for thou dost not mind the things of God, but those of men" (Matt. 16:21-23).

4.

On Three of Jesus' Words on the Cross (John 19:25-30)

The last words of a dying man are sacred. How much more the words of our Lord and Master at the time He was delivering up His life to His Father with full lucidity of mind and perfect generosity of heart!

The scene: "Now there were standing by the cross of Jesus his mother and his mother's sister, Mary of Cleophas, and Mary Magdalene." Let us add: John was also there, witness and reporter, actor and historian in this divine drama. Let us consider the body of our Lord, already overwhelmed by the anguish of death, battered with blows, burning with fever, His blood dripping to the ground. Night is falling, soldiers are on watch nearby, and the comparative silence is broken now and then by a few cries in the distance.

1) "When Jesus, therefore, saw his mother and the disciple standing by, whom he loved, he said to his mother 'Woman, behold, thy son.' Then he said to the disciple, 'Behold, thy mother.' And from that hour the disciple took her into his home" (John 19:26-27).

In this short yet sublime scene, the filial Heart of Jesus is revealed and recapitulated. He has surrendered everything — His body, His reputation, His life work — to the malice of men, but He refuses to abandon His Mother. She is in His thoughts to the very last. He has kept one disciple for Himself, only one, destined to remain faithful even on Calvary. And He has done this so that He may entrust Mary to him. It is also so that in the person of John our whole race may receive Mary as its mother, and so that she may adopt us. Like John, "we take her into our home." She reigns there as Queen and Mistress. She will make up for whatever we lack.

2) "After this Jesus, knowing that all things were now accomplished, that the Scripture might be fulfilled, said, 'I thirst.' " (John 19:28). There is a vessel full of vinegar standing nearby, the bitter drink of the soldiers. One of the soldiers soaks a sponge in the vinegar, puts it on a stalk of hyssop, and applies it to our Lord's lips. A gesture of compassion by this miserable, coarse man. An exemplary gesture. The thirst of Jesus is different from the bodily thirst which He expresses. He thirsts that the kingdom of His Father may come, that His blood may bear fruit, that souls may be purified and saved.

We can, we must make the same gesture as the soldier. We are here to quench the thirst of the Lord. How can we do it? We have only rough instruments, feeble means: a little vinegar, an improvised gadget. And yet we can quench His thirst. For that is precisely what the apostolate is. The human instrument is put into play, and through it God works and converts, fecundates and redeems.

3) "Therefore, when Jesus had taken the wine, he said, 'It is consummated!' And bowing his head, he gave up his spirit" (John 19:30). Please God, may we also be able to say in our last moment that we have done our full duty. To this end, let us pray to Mary to give us fidelity, joy, and fraternal charity, love of her Son and trust in her.

The Preferences of Jesus

The tastes and preferences of Jesus are revealed to us by His life, and St. Paul has formulated them in an admirable way (cf. Phil. 2:5 ff.). Paul takes care to note that he is speaking of the sentiments of Christ: "Have this mind in you which was also in Christ Jesus." Moreover, the Pauline formula agrees in all respects with the evangelical formulas, with the declarations of Christ Himself.

The attitudes that Jesus chose in preference to all others for the accomplishment of the Redemption may be reduced to two: 1) He humbled Himself to the rank of a servant; 2) He obeyed.

Saint Paul reminds us that inasmuch as Christ was by nature God He did not think it usurpation to consider Himself equal to God. And John tells us before his account of the washing of the feet that Jesus knew "that he had come forth from God and was going to God" (John 13:3); that He was rightly called Master and Lord (cf. John 13:13).

This is Jesus' point of departure, the loftiest conceivable, so lofty that it is beyond our comprehension. From the beginning, He is God.

And now comes His gesture, His movement: "[Christ Jesus] emptied himself, taking the nature of a slave" (Phil. 2:7). He empties Himself, He humbles Himself in the greatest measure possible. He takes on the form of a

slave. And He expresses this fact unequivocally: "The
Son of Man has not come to be served but to serve" (Matt.
20:28). From the beginning of His human life, He kneels
at the feet of everyone. The fundamental abasement is the
Incarnation itself: "The Word was made flesh, and dwelt
among us" (John 1:14).

This is Jesus' first preference. If anyone wants to take
on His tastes, well then he must humble himself, he must
serve. That is the whole purpose of our life. We must consider those portions of our apostolate that involve abasement and humiliation not only as quite normal but as deliberately willed, chosen, and loved, as conforming to our
tastes, which have become the tastes of Christ. After all,
we are not gods. What is our abasement compared to His?

The other complementary attitude that Christ wills and
practices is obedience, submission: "He humbled himself,
becoming obedient to death, even to death on a cross"
(Phil. 2:8). That goes far. Jesus obeys His Mother, He
obeys Joseph, He obeys the Law, but above all He obeys
the will of His Father. And this will finds expression for
Him in a chalice full of lethal bitterness: death, death on
a cross. Jesus allows repugnance to overcome Him, to cast
Him into an agony, to put Him under the winepress. But
in all this, He says: "not my will but thine be done" (Luke
22:42). He will obey to death, even to that death.

The great stumbling block, the great obstacle to doing
the right thing, the better thing, is the spirit of independence and pride masquerading under the name of autonomy. This is true especially of souls of some stature
that have a degree of mastery over their sensibilities.

For our part, we want to obey like Jesus, because we
want to take on His sentiments and His tastes. We want
to become as children in order to enter the Kingdom. We
want obedience to dominate our life. But ours must be
real obedience, the obedience of Jesus. It cannot be a passive, automatic, Prussian submission, the obedience of the
obdurate, the callous, the brutish, the obedience of the

heart of stone; the servile obedience of a cowering dog, of a servant who avenges himself through irony, whispered criticisms, and silly prattle about his forced submission.

Ours is the obedience of the living, of the *heart of flesh,* the obedience of sons. It is smiling and supernatural, full of initiative and love. It is founded on the acknowledged identity between the commands and recommendations of obedience on the one hand and the will of God on the other; and also on voluntary sacrifice, on the surrender, the immolation of what is most precious — and most dangerous — to us: attachment to our own judgment and our own interests.

To take on the sentiments of Christ is to strive to do what is best and to love what is best; it is to obey and to delight in obeying: "Yes, Father, for such was thy good pleasure" (Matt. 11:26).

Note on Interior Peace

An essential point in the common life is to maintain an habitual atmosphere of calm, serenity, and practical trust in God. This means that certain attitudes are absolutely out of order: for instance, overly human eagerness, outward agitation, expressions like: "We'll never finish this in time!" "Let's get this done fast!" obvious, noisy improvisations, and the like.

A few practical rules. When very pressed for time, take a few moments to reflect and pray. That is a way of saving a great deal of time.

When it is not possible to do everything, do the most important peacefully, and then *God will provide.* Above all, never get into a feverish excitement or agitation, for that is useless and exhausting.

Maintain — and if necessary, restore — a spirit of interior peace through prayer, by a visit to the Blessed Sacrament, etc. Never deliberately remain under the domination of an interior agitation that is disturbing, impassioned.

Never become an apostle or a peddler of discontent by talking to others with emotion and irritation of abuses, deficiencies, especially to third parties and in the presence of young people. Speak of such things only to God and to your superiors.

Do not feed this turbid flame, especially if it already contains a sentiment, an element of bitterness or revolt, by throwing in the wood of your own reflections, the embers of past emotions, the coals of recriminations, etc.

Interior peace is the *condition of union with God.* Whence its great importance.

Suggested Reading

Psalms 120, 126.

The Imitation of Christ, Book III, Chapters 34, 37, and 54.

Stabat Mater Dolorosa (From the Mass of Our Lady of Sorrows).

Veni Sancte Spiritus.

At that time Jesus spoke and said, "I praise thee, Father, Lord of heaven and earth, that thou didst hide these things from the wise and prudent [according to the flesh], and didst reveal them to little ones. Yes, Father, for such was thy good pleasure . . . . Come to me, all you who labor and are burdened, and I will give you rest. Take my yoke upon you, and learn from me, for I am meek and humble of heart; and you will find rest for your souls" (Matt. 11:25-29).

VI

THE CALL TO THE APOSTOLIC LIFE

1.

Jesus Leaves His Mother To Enter The Apostolic Life

John the Baptist has already begun to preach. Jesus' hour will soon ring, for the dawn announces the day (cf. Matt. 3:1-6). Jesus tells the news to His Mother, who has been living alone with Him since the death of Joseph. Their sweet intimacy must not be broken, or even interrupted. It will simply be deprived of the sensible elements that nourished it. Every apostolic life involves these separations, farewells, and sacrifices. And God metes them out with infinite delicacy according to our strength and to our call.

Jesus hears the apostolic call ring out in His heart. First of all, it is the call of His Father. It is His *vocation:* "For this is why I have been sent" (Luke 4:43).

Let us try to grasp the nobility of this vocation, its divine significance. Provided it is genuine and freely accepted, it makes all sacrifices seem light: "For this is why I have been sent." I have not been sent for this or that reason, not for my pleasure or my repose in creatures, but for one thing only: "This is why I have been sent."

It is also *the call of souls:* "But seeing the crowds, he was
moved with compassion for them, because they were be-
wildered and dejected, like sheep without a shepherd"
(Matt. 9:36). They have masters, they have created their
own masters. Who does not have one? But these souls
(and how many there are like them in our own time) have
no shepherd. They have not found the true and only Master,
the One to whom we say: *Tu solus sanctus, Tu solus Dominus . . . Jesu Christe.*

Mary hears the echo of these calls in her heart. She
has her part to play in all this, and it consists first of all
in not opposing her Son's departure, in letting Him go
where He must go.

The farewells of Mother and Son. Mary will remain alone
from now on. She will see Him only in passing, in hasty
meetings. Souls will compete with her for Him, and they
will win out. They will take Him from her altogether, and
return Him to her dead. Let us savor the admirable and
serene generosity of the Heart of Mary, accepting her
sacrifice without reservation. Let us offer our own sufferings and those that our vocation will impose on others,
especially our family. May this suffering sanctify them
and be their glory and their eternal happiness. For our
part, as we face the tasks of this coming year let us say
with Jesus: "Behold, I come to do thy will, O God" (Heb.
10:9).

Note on Mental Prayer

All mental prayer is not meditation. We are often unable
to meditate because of fatigue, a mental block, spiritual
trials, distractions, absorption with our work. But we can
always pray mentally. We cannot meditate constantly, but
we can engage in continual mental prayer. Why? Because
meditation implies a rather complex intellectual labor demanding a certain repose and freedom of spirit. On the
other hand mental prayer per se requires only a disposition
of will, whether infused or acquired (usually it is a com-
bination of the two), and an affection of the heart.

Mental prayer is conversation, habitual and loving discourse with God, with the interior Master. This discourse, this conversation is of two sorts: it may be *actual,* that is, mental prayer in the strict sense, carried on distinctly, consciously. Meditation comes under this category. It is one of the forms, the intellectual form of mental prayer. There is also *virtual* prayer, the habitual disposition of the heart, mind, and will to hear and obey the voice of the interior Master, the guidance of the Holy Spirit. It is docility to God.

Actual prayer consists in deliberately placing ourselves and remaining for a specified time in the presence of God, seeking divine inspiration, and conforming our life to God's intentions. Divine help to this end is never lacking. We enter actual mental prayer through recollection, through vocal or silent prayer, through the use of our imagination, our memory, or our will. We may pursue a series of considerations tending to convert us, to make us holier, to unite us more closely to God. And that is meditation. Actual mental prayer may also consist in an over-all view of one of the mysteries in the life of our Lord Jesus Christ, of the Blessed Virgin Mary, or of the saints. That is imaginative contemplation. Actual mental prayer may also take the form of simple attention to a mystery or to the details of a mystery. That is the application of the senses. We may apply our senses, for example, to the modesty of the Blessed Virgin, to her simplicity.

Finally, actual mental prayer may consist in a union of presence, a general and indistinct union perhaps to the goodness of God present within us. This may be accompanied by intermittent ejaculatory prayers recalling this goodness, care being taken to push everything else out of the mind. That is the prayer of simplicity.

Now all these forms of actual mental prayer are good at the right time and in obedience to divine inspiration. Negatively, we might say that actual mental prayer is characterized by the deliberate rejection of every other

occupation that is not God Himself or that is not directed
to Him. Positively, it is a conversation with God that has
been deliberately sought and willed.

Virtual prayer, by comparison with actual prayer, is a
feeble and even empty state of mental activity. It consists
in a state of feeling, a voluntary and affective state that
is only intermittently conscious and that can be engaged
in simultaneously with an entirely different and engrossing mental activity. This state is characterized by the following qualities: habitual abnegation of egoism and self-
interest, or at least the deliberate intention of rejecting
selfish attitudes; habitual acceptance of the divine, Christian, apostolic point of view; habitual docility in following
the inspirations that flow from the latter point of view.
In short, it is deliberate and definitive love of the service
and glory of God above our own temporal, human, carnal,
and narrowly circumscribed advantage.

This fundamental disposition is virtually a prayer because it turns us toward the divine Sun much as a sun-
flower is drawn toward the physical sun. The instant a
ray of divine light shines forth strong, distinct, and visible,
it immediately touches the soul. And such rays are always
beaming, for God is constantly pleased with a soul that is
turned toward Him. In consequence there is an uninterrupted exchange, a real conversation, even if not heard
or consciously shared in by us.

Virtual prayer is the disposition that makes us friends
of God, "daughters of God" (the way Joan of Arc was),
capable of being "taught of the Lord" (Is. 54:13). It is
the wellspring of great peace, the condition of a fruitful
apostolate.

The End of Man

Here is a fundamental truth: man is created to praise
God, to honor and serve Him. That is our essential purpose. Every object is known and judged in terms of its
purpose. A key is meant to lock and unlock doors. Beauti-

ful as it may be, if it does not work it has failed its purpose. Conversely, although it may be very crude, if it works that is enough. A plane is built to fly, and to fly fast under certain specified conditions. It may be handsome, shining, and of superb design, but it serves no purpose if it does not fly fast and according to specifications. Well, our fundamental purpose as men is to praise God and to serve Him.

We must praise Him because we are spirits, and hence conscious beings, reflecting glory upon our Maker like good mirrors:

"I have received everything from Thee, and I want to return everything to Thee, without keeping anything for myself, without ever taking back anything."[1]

We must serve Him because we are active beings, and hence capable of exerting influence. Our activity must do honor to our Father, our Master, our End.

If we fail to achieve this primary purpose, we are lost. "For behold, they who go far from thee, shall perish, thou destroyest all who are disloyal to thee" (Ps. 72:27). If we fail, we are lost for God, lost by Him. It is one and the same thing. We fail in our purpose. It is a painful thing to fail in attaining one's goal. A trip may be useful. We arrive at the station too late. It's no use. The train is pulling out. An examination is useful. If we fail it, the consequences may be serious. But it is quite another thing to fail in our purpose in life. There is no way to make up for that. If I fail to attain my purpose in life, I shall be failing not for a day or a year, but for all eternity. And not for myself only but for all those to whom my destiny is linked spiritually.

"O Lord, I am thy servant, and the son of thy handmaid" (Wisd. 9:5).

---

[1] Translation of the *Suscipe* by St. Ignatius.

My Disordered Passions

The essential is to attain my end. And my end is to possess God by means — if I dare say so — of praising, serving, and loving Him. Can anything prevent me from doing it? Yes. Disordered attachment to what is not God or the service of God. To put it briefly, my disordered passions.

My passions are powerful, deep-seated inclinations. They are governable of course, otherwise I would not be a responsible person. But they must be governed by political persuasion, not by despotic methods. I have to reckon with them. I can no more destroy them than I can destroy my own soul. Let us not compare our passions to colors or odors that deeply impregnate the fabric of our life. That does not go far enough. Our passions are incorporated into our life the way colors are imbedded in the clay of porcelains. The only way to annihilate them is to break the vase.

My passions are not all unruly. Love of God, love of souls, disinterested zeal are completely good passions. But the fact remains that my deep-rooted passions, before their conquest by grace, before I have succeeded in purifying them with God's help, are all without exception sullied by a primordial disorder. It is the threefold disorder that inclines me spontaneously toward pride, egoism, and sensuality. In this initial state my passions are untamed and restive forces. They are like wild young horses, great felines, raging torrents. When left to themselves they follow their own bent, and, impatient with regulation and restriction, catapult down the inevitable road of self-love.

That is the enemy.

Do I have these passions? Yes, certainly. If I do not know them, it is because they are already in great part dominated by graces of divine preservation or because they have been sublimated, subtilized, and have assumed less violent forms that mislead me as to their virulence.

The truth is that I have an evil self — a haughty, pleasure-seeking, egoistical and perverse self, a self that is sluggish or passionate, plaintive or domineering, groveling or arrogant, depending on my temperament or my past. These evil forces are always obscure because they are profoundly intertwined with my temperament, my senses, indeed my very body. In dealing with them, I am in the position of a man facing a great aroused feline. Either die or kill!

There are three possible attitudes to take in dealing with the passions:

1) Surrender almost without a fight. That is slavery to the passions. Alas! many men choose this solution, and in the measure that they surrender they are off the path that leads to their last end. "They who go far from thee shall perish" (Ps. 72:27).

2) Resist and conquer, not without a struggle but without any voluntary, deliberately accepted compromise. That is the guarantee of a life habitually united to God, a good, pure life fruitful in spiritual riches. Those who have reached this stage are on the path that leads to their last end.

3) Delay, negotiate, resist on one point and yield on another, bridle sensuality and unleash jealousy, drive out vanity and retain a spirit of criticism; overcome sloth and tolerate vain self-satisfaction; combat anger and play with gluttony. In short, live by compromise. This third attitude is the one that we need to fear. A hundred times we have anathematized the first, while adopting and praising the second. A hundred times we have found ourselves practicing the third.

What, then, are we to do? St. Ignatius answers: There must be a joining of forces. Experience shows that passion, though it begins as an allurement, tends to end as a maxim, a theoretical affirmation. If we keep doing something long enough, we will in the end justify it. We start

out by being the victim of our passion, and end by being
its dupe and apologist.

The right method to follow is to reverse this trend, and
re-establish, revive, regain an ever-clearer, more explicit,
and more vigorous view of our life's purpose and of the
extent to which our passions jeopardize its attainment. We
must therefore keep always before us the thought of what
we must do to subjugate, canalize, and turn to a good
end these rebellious forces within us that are innately
oriented in the wrong direction.

That is our intellectual obligation with regard to our
passions. It varies in difficulty and importance, but it is
always important and difficult. The time for this effort is
now. Our meditations are directed toward this goal, but
that is not enough. After we have reoriented our sentiments, we must inspire and nourish them. To control the
flow of the torrent, we must feed it frequently, and discover
brooklets that will make of it a river, a stream of life,
instead of a devastating scourge. To this end, it will help
us to keep in mind the example and the love of our Lord
Jesus Christ and of His Mother, above all by the exercise
that St. Ignatius calls "the application of the senses."

Returning Everything to God

My end, my only end is to praise God, to serve Him.
And this is to save my soul. In turn it means that I must
help save others along with myself.

A real obstacle: my disordered passions. And it is a fact
that I have such passions.

A method to overcome this obstacle: the Ignatian
method, so wise, at once so human and so supernatural.
A method that does justice to the whole man, to my intelligence and to my emotions.

A light, a passion, a passion that is all pure and good.

The light is an intellectual power opposed to my disordered passions. I must realize that nothing has any value for me except in relation to my one and only end. That applies to the things of this world, even to persons insofar as they intervene in my life, as well as to providential circumstances that touch me or completely engulf me — circumstances of health, comfort, sickness, weakness, poverty, success, esteem, humiliation, and so on. A priori, I must consider all these things as indifferent, as matter with which to serve God, as means of praising Him. From all this wood I can make an arrow. My duty, therefore, is to dominate circumstances, to control them by my thought, to see them in their proper perspective. It is necessary to foresee in order to accomplish. Before Colonel Goethals resumed the work of completing the Panama Canal he spent a year, with the help of doctors and public health experts, setting up methods and services necessary to conquer yellow fever. He paid no attention to the ridicule and criticism heaped upon him by outsiders. Time devoted to a calm and serene inspection of facts is time spent in the best possible way.

Yes, the astonishingly different alternatives that may face me can all help me to attain my end or turn me away from it. It matters not whether they are attractive or repugnant: comfort, poverty, health, sickness, success, failure, general esteem, scorn. They can all help or hinder me, whether pleasant or painful. Out of this raw material I can draw the strength to attain my end, not just by a hair's breadth but fully, gloriously.

Confidence, therefore! But on the other hand, I must not be like the man who wants coal that will not blacken his hands, and scented wood for his fireplace. I want coal that heats, wood that burns. I am indifferent to the rest.

Light is indispensable. But after all, I am not a brain living in pure oxygen. I am a being who feels, wills, and loves. How can I make use of this power to attain my end? By loving powerfully "unice eligendo et desiderando,"

by loving with a jealous and in a sense exclusive love this
very end that is mine.

It is not a material end: a mountain to climb, so that
I may enjoy the magnificent view from its summit. It is
not a human end: a house where I shall be with those I love
in peace and joy. It is not a temporary end: it is not for
ten years, a hundred years, a lifetime. It is a divine end.
It is to see supreme Beauty, to love indefectible Goodness, to delight in boundless Love. My end is to love God!
If we love Him as we should, then the rest will matter
only in the measure that it leads us to Him. The rest
will seem bad to us only in the measure that it separates
us from Him. Everything is good that gives me my Love,
everything is bad that separates me from Him, that draws
me away from Him, that exiles me from Him.

Suggested Reading

Psalm 85, Incline thy ear, O Lord, hear me . . . .

Psalm 90, You who dwell in the shelter of the Most High . . . .

Imitation of Christ, Book III, Chapters 1 and 9.

God, my Father, who exhort to prayer and who grant what
is asked of you, hear this poor creature that I am, groping
his way in the darkness, hold out your hand to me! Send your
Light before me, draw me back from the paths of error: so
that guided by you I may return to myself, I may return to
you! (Saint Augustine, *Soliloq.,* 12, 6).

I love you, Lord! Love, ardor, fervor. Beneath my feet, all
delectation! I want to pass! O to love, to go forward, to die to
myself, to reach you! (Saint Augustine, *Sermo* 159, 8).

2.

The Presentation in the Temple

This contemplation offers us immense vistas. There is
enough here to meditate upon for a week or more. We
shall touch on only a few points. Concentrate on the point
which impresses you most, as the instinct of the Holy Spirit
inspires you.

The Law of Moses demanded that the firstborn son of every family be offered in a special way to the Lord, as a firstfruit. And this son had to be redeemed by a sacrifice. For the poor folk and those of moderate means like Joseph and Mary, the offering consisted of two pigeons or two young turtledoves. We see the Holy Family going up to the Temple. Mary is carrying her beloved Child with infinite respect and love. Joseph is holding the little basket with the turtledoves.

Jesus is offered by His Mother. She knows, even before Simeon's prophecy, the significance of this offering. She knows she is holding a victim in her arms. But she also sees the fruit of Jesus' sacrifice. At least she sees it in its broad outlines, has a presentiment of it, guesses it. She delights in the bitter and holy will of God for her Son, freely choosing this bloody and fraternal redemption.

Joseph does not think so far ahead. He knows only that what is happening is a divine work, and hence a good, holy, and sacred work. He strengthens his resolution to help in it with his whole heart, with all his strength, and with all his love. He repeats to himself: *Serviam!* I will serve!

Simeon's prophecy. It is so majestic, so touching. In the *Nunc dimittis* the fundamental truth is powerfully expressed: man's whole purpose is to carry out the role that God has assigned to him. When this role has been accomplished, then everything is done: "Now thou dost dismiss thy servant" (Luke 2:29). Next, the work of the Redemption and of the apostolate is described in compelling terms: Jesus is the artisan of universal salvation, He is salvation itself, "thy salvation," salvation sent by God. Salvation for the Gentiles, salvation for Israel. The apostolate is the only efficacious means of sharing in this eternal and supreme work.

Then the words addressed directly to Mary, and the twin prophecies: ". . . this child is destined . . . for a sign that shall be contradicted" (Luke 2:34). It is with regard to

Jesus that the great division will occur between those who choose the Light and those who prefer the darkness, between the sheep and the goats, between the humble and the proud.

And finally, like a dagger thrust: "And thy own soul a sword shall pierce" (Luke 2:35). For Mary will be present at the great judgment that will be accomplished through the Passion and Crucifixion; and the tragic conditions of this mystery will impinge upon her Son only by passing through her. In this role she will be the Co-Redemptrix of men, united at an unbelievable depth to the oblation of her Son. She will be the Mother and succor of sinners, the refuge of the wicked who want to become good again, the strength of the weak who need to be strong.

Hail Mary. . . .

Hail, holy Queen. . . .

The Abasements of Christ

At the conclusion of the first Exercise on sin, St. Ignatius suggests to his retreatant a twofold colloquy, two very simple conversations, one with Christ and the other with himself.

In the presence of Christ crucified, the retreatant is to ask Him how He was induced to leave His eternal and glorious repose as the Word of God, and take on a servile human nature, thus pledging Himself to become entangled in a temporal life, in our life of misery and suffering; and to walk to the end of this valley of tears, to its very depths, even to death, and death on a Cross.

Jesus: I shall teach you what sin is. I have deliberately accepted this unbelievable abasement for you and for your sins. Do you want to know what my Father thinks of sin, of your sin? For it is your sin because you committed it and also because, in the measure that you did not commit it, it was my blood that preserved you from it, not your courage; it was my pure mercy, not your wavering will.

Well, to redeem this sin, to make reparation for it, to wipe it out, my Father thought it just to deliver me up even to the Cross: "God [so hated sin that he] sent his only-begotten Son into the world" (I John 4:9). You can judge sin from that.

Against sin there are the punishments of this life: sufferings, sicknesses, separations, difficulties, uncertainties, agonies. But that is not enough! Against sin there is hell, the destiny of the damned, the terrible words: "I know you not." That is not enough, for the glory of the Infinite One demands an infinite reparation. In a sense, of course, it is too much, for this terrible justice is not illumined with enough mercy. What else is there?

There is abasement, the form of the slave, the "appearing in the form of man" (Phil. 2:7), the "Word made flesh." *Flesh!* Almost-nothingness, infirm element, "omnis caro foenum"! And I shall become that — I the only-begotten Son, the Beloved, pure Spirit! And by this "emptying," by this supreme abasement, by the assumption of this body of sin, I shall become the homage of powerless humanity, its contrition, its repentance, its reparation. "Because of you and because of your sins. . . ."

What other reason do I have? Because I love you. Know thereby what my Father thinks of the sinner that you are: God so loved the sinner that He gave His only-begotten Son. Whence this extraordinary love? From the fact that you are my creature. Think of the affection that you have, wretched man, for all that you have made, for the plant you have cultivated, for the lamb, the dove you have raised, the child for whom you have sacrificed yourself. You become attached in the measure that you give yourself, and that is a beautiful reflection of my creative love.

I have given you everything. You are not my chosen plant, my favorite flock, my privileged child. You are my *creature*. Everything you have comes from me. Without me you would not exist, without me you would be nothing.

I am your Alpha and Omega, your absolute origin, your
last end. That is why, notwithstanding your great and
fathomless misery, my Father loves you. *"For God so loved
the world that he gave his only-begotten Son"* (John 3:16).

In the matter of redeeming you, a condonation could
have sufficed. It was not enough for me. An intervention
on my part, a word, an attitude, a cry from my human
nature sufficed. That was not enough for me. I wanted to
go to the end, to enter the darkness, to go and look for you
in your brambles, wash you from your impurities, and nurse
the disgusting wounds of the old Adam.

Contempt for Self

The second colloquy that St. Ignatius suggests to his
retreatant regarding sin is a colloquy with himself. The
purpose of this interior conversation is to induce him to take
his rightful place: "colloquium instituere inspiciendo meip-
sum: quid egerim ego pro Christo, quid agam, quid agere
debeam." "To make a colloquy in which I look at myself,
asking what I have done for Christ, what I am doing for
Christ, what I ought to do for Christ."

In all the Exercises of the first week, notably the second
on personal sins, which includes this colloquy, St. Ignatius
gives precious recommendations to facilitate this task. It
is a matter of learning to know oneself in order to fulfill the
preliminary condition for all profound union with God.
This condition is a certain contempt for self.

Both Scripture and experience teach us that the gift of
fear is the first of the gifts of the Holy Spirit. They teach
that it is fundamental, "the beginning of wisdom" (Ps. 110:
10). They show us that when the supernatural takes hold
of a man he humbles himself in his nothingness. (Consider Jeremias, St. Elizabeth, St. Peter, St. Paul, etc.) Even
great actions on a strictly human level make analogous
demands. A man who does not hold his time, his health, his
very life cheap will never be a hero. Now, when we hold

ourselves cheap we are acting as if we scorned our own well-being, our health, our life.

But to be truly united to God, it is not enough to act "as if." "Man seeth those things that appear, but the Lord beholdeth the heart" (1 Kings 16:7). Hence it is absolutely indispensable that we have sincere contempt for self, or at least an initial will to self-contempt. God will always respond to our effort by a greater effusion of the gift of fear.

Self-contempt leaves room within us for grace. It accomplishes the necessary work of pruning and demolition. It makes us accept indispensable humiliations. By thinning down our pride it enables us to pass through the narrow gate which alone gives access to the kingdom of heaven. To facilitate this difficult task and to help us attain our goal, St. Ignatius multiplies his recommendations during the first week of the Exercises. Here are a few of his hints.

In the prelude to the first Exercise he invites us to think of our soul as imprisoned in our corruptible body, and of our whole being as exiled in a gross and bestial environment. These are the very thoughts and words of St. Paul (cf. Rom. 7:14-25). Our soul has wonderful impulsions. But alas! it is imprisoned. It is like a high-flying bird held in a dirty, narrow cage where he cannot even spread his crumpled and vermin-ridden wings. How often does our corruptible and corruptive body thwart, weigh down, and enchain our efforts to soar. We would like to work, to serve, to advance in knowledge, in the apostolate, in the gift of self, in abnegation, in union with God. We half-open our wings. And we are bruised, soiled, by the indigence, the wretched wants of our body.

Besides, it is not only the body that deserves contempt. It would be too beautiful to play the role of a princess imprisoned in a dungeon. Let us not allow our imagination to feed on this false, romantic vision. St. Ignatius reminds us in the third point of the Second Exercise that we must consider ourselves, both body and soul, as a sort of ulcer, a

hideous and revolting sore from which all manner of in-
fection can erupt.

And in fact do not our vile intrigues of self-love, our
insincerity, our maneuvers to attract attention, our affec-
tionate liberties, our indiscretions, our cruel, impudent,
murderous words, our desired, savored sensualities, our
gross acts of egoism — do they not make a veritable dunghill? And the worst part of all this is the spiritual. The
most putrid corruption exudes not from our fleshly wrapping but from our inner corruption, from our proud or sensual perversity. When we realize this, self-contempt raises
its head and we begin to have a sense of shame. Let us
not blink or close our eyes. Let us not turn away too
quickly. Each of us can say: that is my image before me.
The mirror does not exaggerate.

And finally there is our environment, the human milieu
in which we live. It is so ugly, monotonous, earthy, bestial.
I am part and parcel of it. It is my flesh and blood. Am
I so far removed from that poor painted girl of the streets?
Is it not a matter of orientation, of training, of divine predilection and preservation? She is my sister in Adam, my
sister in initial corruption. My place as a human being is
here among the beasts, in this trainful of coarse, swearing
people.

Such being the case, what gratitude I owe to the One
who came to lift me up from my dunghill: "He . . . raises up
the poor from the dunghill, that he may set him with
princes" (Ps. 112:7).

Contempt for self does not take away courage.

The Consecrated Man

As men, we have an end to attain. If we fail, it is irreparable. The essential thing is to attain it. The rest
matters little or not at all. As apostles, as consecrated men,
we have an end to attain. Our vow consecrates us. What

does this mean if not that it unites us as hosts to the great Victim of Calvary, to Jesus-*Hostia?*

What are the ends to which a host is destined? The ends of sacrifice.

A host *adores*. That is, by the very state in which it is placed, by its state of sacrifice, of offering, of oblation, it recognizes the sovereign dominion of God. The consecrated person adores in body and mind, in spirit and in truth. Of what value is a consecrated person who adores only in appearance? "And the Lord said: this people with their lips glorify me, but their heart is far from me" (Is. 29:13). A consecrated man whose heart is distracted, absent, divided? Such a man belies his exterior profession by his life. He is turning his back on his end.

A host *makes reparation*. That is, by the very state in which it is placed, it is a living atonement, a protestation, a supplication. It is there for those who are not! It is in this state to raise the level of moral and spiritual life, to counterbalance, to offset sins — his own sins and those of others. Of what use is a consecrated person who does not make reparation but on the contrary increases his own and others' debts by his laxity, his sensuality, his pride, his lies? He weighs down the scales of justice, he draws down God's anger.

A host *gives thanks*. By its very state of sacrifice, it says: "Amen, so be it. It is good. Yea, Father. . . ." Regardless of appearances, trials, and darkness, it cries out: "All is well, all is for love!" (Blessed Juliana of Norwich). What then is a consecrated person who complains of everything, of himself, his superiors, his assignment, his health, even of Providence? What is a consecrated person who says: "So be it not! Nothing is good. What is truth?" He is completely lost, he is turned away from his end.

A host *implores* and obtains favors from God. By its very state of sacrifice, by its innocence, it is an efficacious word, a pleasing voice, a supplication that is heard, a filial cry, a living prayer. What then is a consecrated person who places himself outside the conditions of his state by his accepted, deliberate, cherished sins; by his search for and pleasure in created things, if not sinful things; temporal, if not carnal things; human, if not diabolic things? He has lost sight of his end. He has turned his back on it.

This sullied, stained, damaged, deformed, gnawed host, displeasing to the One for whom alone it exists, must be restored to its whiteness, its purity, its full beauty.

Is such a thing possible? Thank God, it is easy. "Behold, the lamb of God, who takes away the sin of the world" (John 1:29).

Suggested Reading

Psalm 31: Blessed is he whose iniquity is forgiven . . . .

Psalm 37: O Lord, rebuke me not in thy anger . . . .

Psalm 50: Have mercy on me, O God . . . .

Imitation of Christ, Book III, Chapters 50 and 52.

. . . and [she] forgot me, saith the Lord. Therefore, behold I will allure her, and will lead her into the wilderness; and I will speak to her heart. . . . And it shall be in that day, saith the Lord, that she shall call me: My husband . . . . And I will espouse thee to me forever: and I will espouse thee to me in justice, and judgment, and in mercy, and in commiserations. And I will espouse thee to me in faith; and thou shalt know that I am the Lord. . . . and I will have mercy on her that was without mercy. And I will say to that which was not my people: Thou art my people. And they shall say: Thou art my God (Osee 2:13-24).

But thanks be to God that you who were the slaves of sin have now obeyed from the heart that form of doctrine into which you have been delivered, and having been set free from sin, you have become the slaves of justice. I speak in a human way because of the weakness of your flesh; for as you yielded your members as slaves of uncleanness and iniquity unto iniquity, so now yield your members as slaves of justice unto sanctification. . . . But now set free from sin and become slaves of God, you have your fruit unto sanctification, and as your end, life everlasting (Rom. 6:17-22).

3.

The Temptations of Christ (Luke 4:1-13)

These temptations are archetypes.

The devil tempts us when we are hungry, tired, devoid of fervor, when we are spiritually and physically weakened.

The first temptation is self-pity — and in Jesus' case how well justified! But Jesus makes use of His miraculous power only for His mission, not for His own well-being.

The second temptation is vertigo (produced by looking out upon the expanses of human glory) and the temptation of intimidation: "for to me they have been delivered, and to whomever I will I give them" (Luke 4:6). Satan is a great fashioner of mirages, a great producer of vertigo, and he strives to intimidate by lies if need be. Jesus' reply "The Lord thy God shalt thou worship, and him only shalt thou serve" (Luke 4:8) is a stone wall against all deception and intimidation.

The third temptation is one of self-satisfaction and presumption. The devil makes a very clever allusion to Scripture: "It is written, *He will give his angels charge concerning thee . . .* " (Luke 4:11).

All these temptations are directed at Jesus the Messias, tending either to divert Him from His mission for selfish reasons, or to deflect His course toward carnal ambition. Our temptations will often be the temptations of apostles, tending to imprison us in our self-love, in our own narrow views.

The devil retreats, but only "for a while" (Luke 4:13). He never withdraws completely.

Note on Penance

Penance has many advantages. St. Ignatius enumerates the three principal ones: satisfaction for past sins; mastery of self, notably the inferior, carnal self; impetration for

graces of light and compassion, etc. These points offered
no problem for the Saint's contemporaries. But for us and
for others, a few words of explanation are not superfluous.

The advantage of penance as satisfaction for past sins
is that it is at once an act of faith and an act of avenging
justice. My senses, my body, which have been the in-
centive to and often the instruments of sin, must be
punished. Thus will total justice be re-established. But in
addition, this gesture, in itself of little worth by comparison
with my sins, deepens and facilitates within me the interior
act of penance, of contrition, of conversion that detaches
from sin and purifies. It also obtains from God a grace of
more complete forgiveness with regard to the temporal
consequences and the deep-lying roots of sin. It goes without saying that this last-named benefit comes to us not by
any automatic action or *opus operatum,* not by merit in the
strict sense, but by a sort of fitness.

The second advantage of penance is so clearly evident
that any psychologist can see it at first glance, and will
counsel mortification of the senses for that reason alone.
It should be noted, however, that among the lower ap-
petites curbed by penance, self-love, pride, and self-satisfaction are mortified quite as much as sensuality itself. And
this is a great good.

The third advantage of penance depends solely on the
good pleasure of God. It is another application of the
principle of fitness (*de congruo* as opposed to *de condigno*)
which plays such a great part in the life of union with God.
It is fitting, it is just in the general sense of the word, it
is proper that God in His mercy should take notice of our
poor efforts. Evidently, it is not a bargain, it is not an
exchange. It is simply a matter of fitness. Such acts performed by a person in the state of grace always obtain
some merit, since they are done for the love of God. But
more than this, even if they are performed by someone in
the state of sin (God forbid!) they "incline" God to mercy.
In other words, they manifest a generous, efficacious good-

will ready to make sacrifice, that is pleasing to God. Experience confirms that the universal sentiment of Christians on this point is founded on fact. In the case of certain graces of contrition and compassion sought by this means, there is also a relationship between the sentiments desired and the penitential practices followed.

The Apostolic Vocation

Christ's call is universal. But it has degrees. All men are called to the salvation brought by Jesus. God wills the salvation of all men. And we are men. An immense number of men are called to save their souls through Christ in a deliberate manner, by knowing that "No one comes to the Father but through me. I am the way, and the truth, and the life" (John 14:6). And we are of their number. This is where the elite begins. As the number of those who are called decreases, the role of divine predilection and of human good will increases.

A considerable number of men are called to save their souls by collaborating actively and consciously with Christ in the salvation of others. These are the apostles. And we are among them. In this chosen group there is also a more limited elite, composed of those who may be called "professional apostles," those who have made the service of Christ the center of their life. They are the ones who free themselves as much as possible from the bonds of human passions, joys, and satisfactions that could hold them back. "Come, follow me, and I will make you fishers of men" (Matt. 4:19). "Master, I will follow thee wherever thou goest" (Matt. 8:19). "If thou wilt be perfect . . . come, follow me" (Matt. 19:21). "What is it to thee? Do thou follow me" (John 21:22). We are included in this group. This is the apostolic vocation in the strong sense of the word.

This vocation is freely given. "You have not chosen me, but I have chosen you, and have appointed you that you should go and bear fruit, and that your fruit should remain. No longer do I call you servants. . . . But I have called you friends" (John 15:16, 15).

This vocation is free, except in certain very rare cases (which are miracles of mercy): "If thou wilt. . . ."

It is made known to us in many different ways. "To him who overcomes, I will give the hidden manna, and I will give him a white pebble, and upon the pebble a new name written, which no one knows except him who receives it" (Apoc. 2:17). There is a secret between the Lord and each one of His elect. The call to Mary is not the call to Martha; Xavier's is not Aloysius de Gonzaga's or Francis de Sales'.

It is a story, already quite long perhaps, written in double entries showing the fidelity of divine predilections and the frailty of the human response. Often I have refused to say: "Yes!" Sometimes I have said "No!" or "Not yet!" or "This is a hard saying." And yet the invitation was a call of love.

There are aspects of this vocation common to all, and these St. Ignatius brings out vividly in his parable on the Kingdom. First, the grandeur of the work and its beauty. What is in question here is nothing less than the extension of the kingdom of God and the salvation of men. The Blood of Christ, infinitely fruitful in virtuality and in power, will produce its fruits in truth and in act in the measure that the work of the apostle is done well or badly, zealously or indifferently. This is the only work directed exclusively and immediately to eternal ends. It is a great thing for a Joan of Arc, for a brave general and his soldiers to liberate their country. In the glory of such an accomplishment the pettiness, the weaknesses, even the crimes of individuals are lost sight of. And yet this is only a temporal matter. To the apostle can be said: "Enlarge the place of thy tent, and stretch out the skins of thy tabernacles. Spare not: lengthen thy cords, and strengthen thy stakes" (Is. 54:2).

Then there is the unique character of the Head, and

therefore of the work which remains personal despite its collective nature. In other works we must make a choice: either carry on as pirates, guerillas, or lose ourselves in a collective mass, abdicate our preferences and become serial numbers, nameless atoms. We cannot choose our leaders. Some are great, almost ideal: for instance, St. Louis of France, St. Joan of Arc. But there are no perfect leaders. Above all, no human leader can know each of his men and live the life of each man. While this may remain a goal to be sought, no one ever comes very close to it.

In the work of the apostolate, it is different. Our Leader knows us. In fact He knows us so well that St. Paul, in trying to give us some notion of the knowledge and joy of the beatific vision, says: "But then I shall know even as I have been known" (1 Cor. 13:12). Our Master knows us perfectly, better than we know ourselves. And knowing us, He calls us. If I were really known, would any human master ever call me? He would see my faults, my failings, my passions. Jesus knows me, and calls me.

In the apostolate, our Leader fights with us. In difficult circumstances men are forced to rise above sentiment, to become hard. Such was the meaning of General de Castelnau's "Let us go on!" when he learned of the death of one of his sons. A man carries his wounded brother to safety, embraces him, and returns to battle. Jesus for His part is always tender.

Jesus does not abandon us. We are never forced to leave Him. We must never leave Him. And He for His part never abandons anyone.

Various Answers to the Call

Those who have the grace and the courage to answer the call of Jesus fully, who give themselves wholeheartedly to labors, must react firmly against hostile forces, forces of contraction and obstruction that would impede their growth. To conquer these forces is the condition of our

progress. And to conquer them, we must know them. That
is all too clear. Otherwise we would be charging blindly,
we would be slaughtered to no purpose.

These forces, St. Ignatius tells us, are of several sorts.
But the ones that must first be efficaciously overcome are
not exterior forces, whether diabolic or human. These are
formidable indeed, but they still form the second line of
the enemy's attack. More often than not the enemy won't
even have to defend this line if his front line holds. Now
the front line is wholly within us, and yet it is very
visible to anyone who will observe carefully. St. Ignatius
designates it by two very explicit names: 1) sensuality;
2) carnal and worldly love. Together, they are like a
double line of barbed wire that shuts us off — inwardly and
initially — from the road of the apostolate, from the service of God upon which we have entered.

First, *sensuality:* "After this [Samson] loved a woman,
who dwelt in the valley of Sorec, and she was called Dalila.
And the princes and the Philistines came to her, and said:
Deceive him, and learn of him wherein his great strength
lieth, and how we may be able to overcome him, to bind and
afflict him: which if thou shalt do, we will give thee everyone of us eleven hundred pieces of silver. And Dalila said to
Samson: Tell me, I beseech thee, wherein thy greatest
strength lieth, and what it is wherewith if you wert bound
thou couldst not break loose. . . . And when she pressed
him much, and continually hung upon him for many days,
giving him no time to rest, his soul fainted away, and was
wearied even until death. Then opening the truth of the
thing, he said to her . . ." (Judg. 16:4-6; 16-17).

Could it be expressed more cogently? Dalila is our
sensuality. Even the greatest, the strongest of men, the
Samsons of the apostolate, Paul, Vincent Ferrer, Xavier,
if they had listened to it, if they had opened their hearts
to its songs, its incantations, would have been lost to the
apostolate. Sensuality would have bound them fast and
delivered them up to every sort of passion. Dalila always

goes about it in the same way. The old means are the good ones. She flatters, she presses, to the point of obtaining from her victim's lassitude what was first refused her.

Sensuality flatters: our love of comfort, our grossest and most subtle tastes, from gluttony to the most refined artistic dilettantism. It invites us to savor — first in thought, in imagination, in regret, in desire, and then in fact — all the pleasures of the senses, those that are permitted, those that are dangerous, those that are forbidden. It places a halo around the forbidden fruit. It adds a more noble savor, and even a vague apostolic aroma to shameful satisfactions and surrenders.

Sensuality presses. It cajoles, hoping to win from our lassitude, our exhaustion, our confusion what it cannot conquer in fair battle. After three feints, Samson yields to the insistence of this perverse woman: "his soul fainted away, and was wearied even until death. Then opening [his heart], he said to her. . . ." This is the most skillful political strategy, against which we must never imagine we are altogether immunized.

Anyone who wants to follow Christ and be a good soldier must not listen to Dalila, compromise with her, argue with her. He would be vanquished. He must drive her out, discourage her, fight her. It must be done without great fanfare but with iron resolution born of love. Dalila is our Master's enemy. She wants to wrest us from His love.

The second enemy is what St. Ignatius calls *carnal and worldly love,* that is to say, the most widespread form of pride: the passion to assert ourselves, to seek attention, to attract and hold the eyes, the admiration, and even the envy of others. In short, it is all that nourishes and encourages worldliness, the desire to cut a figure and to excel. This enemy is formidable because its action is self-centered, centripetal, spiderlike, and essentially opposed to generous expansion, self-giving, self-forgetfulness, abandonment, simplicity, humiliation, and self-contempt.

It is an evil servant who follows us everywhere with a
mirror, inviting us to look at ourselves, to preen, to pity
ourselves, to see everything and everyone — both ourselves and others — reflected in it. Thus it keeps us from
ever looking at our heavenly models, our guiding stars, the
saints, the Blessed Virgin, our Lord. For in this mirror
these exemplars appear only as quivering, confused images,
their proportions distorted by our own ever-present image.
Worldly pride is a tireless servant. It follows us into our
cell, to the chapel, deep into the woods, by the sea, into our
family and community, and into solitude. As long as we
have not rejected it, discouraged it, scorned it, bullied it,
it will be there.

Anyone who wants to follow Christ must drive out
pride cold-bloodedly, resolutely, perseveringly. Above all
he must replace it and choose a different mirror, the Mirror
of Justice.

The Annunciation

Anyone who wants to follow Jesus the King seriously,
to work with Him and through Him for the expansion of
the kingdom of God, must mortify his sensual and worldly
self, his excessive desire for pleasant sensations and expressions of esteem and honor. We must send Dalila away,
drive off the little mirror-carrying dwarf. We have already
tried to convince ourselves of this. But as Quintilian says
very aptly: "Precepts make the road long, but examples
make it short and easy."

That is why it is supremely important to look upon our
models, Mary and Jesus. That is why the major portion of
the second week of the *Exercises* is dedicated by St. Ignatius to the contemplation of the life of Christ. But Ignatius
never forgets the Mother. In fact this is what distinguishes
his spirituality most sharply from that of the author of the
Imitation, so similar to his on many points.

Let us, therefore, briefly consider the Annunciation of
the Blessed Virgin Mary. We probably know the text by

heart: "Now in the sixth month [after the conception of St. John the Baptist] the angel Gabriel was sent from God to a town of Galilee called Nazareth, to a virgin betrothed to a man named Joseph . . . and the virgin's name was Mary. And when the angel had come to her, he said, 'Hail, full of grace . . .' " (Luke 1:26-28).

Mary is praying, recollected, alone. What is her prayer? Its essence is surely "Thy kingdom come" tempered by "Thy will be done," which in that day is summed up in the words "Send forth, O Lord, the Lamb, the ruler of the earth" (Is. 16:1). Her mode of prayer? The simplest imaginable: a profound, respectful intimacy, the abandonment of a child who has never offended her Father, who looks to Him as the only Master, the only Lord, the Most High, a child who delights in Him with no thought of self: "she did not please herself" (cf. Rom. 15:3).

The angel converses with the Virgin and tells her: You are to be the Mother of God! The Son of David, whom David was inspired to call his Lord, the Prophet upon whom the Spirit will rest in plenitude, God, the Strong One, the Prince of the world to come, the Servant of the Most High who will redeem His brothers by His death and His sufferings, the Vinedresser whose garments are crimson with blood, Emmanuel who is to bring God into our midst will be Mary's Son. How? By the powerful, secret, mysterious action of the Holy Spirit.

Mary's sentiments: I, the Mother of the Messias? A glance within herself, a lightning flash but so penetrating! I who am nothingness, a creature, I, Mary — am I "the one" that every Jewish maiden aspires to be in her loftiest dreams? Am I to be the mother of "the One who is to come"?

The angel waits. The message must have an answer. Nothing has been done so far. God respects Mary's free will by asking her consent. Then a glance at the future here on earth: the joys, the sorrows, the Child, the Prophet, the Man of Sorrows, the unforeseen, Joseph.

God invites, God calls. The rest is nothing. "Behold
the handmaid of the Lord." Simply, without mental reser-
vations, without recall, for happiness and misfortune, for
herself and for others, at God's good pleasure, at the mercy
of God, "Behold the handmaid of the Lord."

And the Word was made flesh.

Suggested Reading

Psalm 64: "A hymn is due to thee, O God . . . ."

Psalm 83: "How lovely is thy dwelling, O Lord of Hosts!"

Imitation of Christ, Book II, Chapters 7 and 8.

Grapes hang on vines, olives on trees, and as long as they
cling to their branches they enjoy the free air, so to speak.
But the grape is not wine, and the olive is not oil before passing under the press. So is it with those whom God has chosen
to be faithful images of His only-begotten Son, of this Son
who surrendered His essence, like an immense bunch of grapes
under the wine press.

If you are one of these chosen ones, you enjoy — before
you consecrate yourself to the service of God — a delightful
independence in the world, as do grapes and olives on their
branches. But since it has been written: "Son, when thou comest
to the service of God, stand in justice and in fear, and prepare thy soul for temptation" (Ecclus. 2:1), you must understand that when you consecrate yourself to the service of God,
you come to the wine press, you will be broken, crushed, pressed,
not for your destruction here on earth but so that, as a heavenly liquor, you may flow into the treasures of God. You will be
stripped of the mantle of your earthly desires, like grapes from
their stems.

But under the wine press [remember that] you are thus
broken because, putting aside your selfish love that drew you
toward worldly, secular, temporal, vain, and perishable things,
through the countless sufferings, tribulations, and temptations
to which this selfish love will impel you in this life, you are
beginning to seek the [heavenly] rest that is not of this life
or of this earth (St. Augustine, in *Psalm* 83:3).

VII

THE LIFE OF FAITH

1.

The Sterile Fig Tree

"A certain man had a fig tree planted in his vineyard; and he came seeking fruit thereon, and found none. And he said to the vine-dresser, 'Behold, for three years now I have come seeking fruit on this fig tree, and I find none. Cut it down, therefore; why does it still encumber the ground?' But he answered him and said, 'Sir, let it alone this year too, till I dig around it and manure it. Perhaps it may bear fruit; but if not, then afterwards thou shalt cut it down'" (Luke 13:6-9).

This text must be read with simplicity of heart, calmly, without anxiety. Our fig tree is not sterile to the point of causing us concern about our salvation. But it may be and no doubt is relatively sterile. And this condition does not befit the apostolic life.

A few points to note: The master of the vineyard comes to see his fig tree at the fruit-bearing season. He is disappointed, astonished. "Behold, for three years now I have come seeking fruit on this fig tree, and I find none."

And what about me?

What he reproaches the fig tree for is not its sterility on that particular day, which might be accidental, but its long-continued sterility. No progress.

What he proposes is to replace the fig tree with a more fruitful one. "Cut that fig tree down! Why should it stand there encumbering the ground?"

Then comes the intercession of the good vine-dresser who loves his whole field, even the poor sterile tree: "Sir, let it alone this year too. I shall spare no effort. I shall dig around it and manure it. Perhaps then it may bear fruit. If not, then so be it!"

Even though our whole tree is not sterile, some of its branches may be.

Colloquy with our Lord, the Master of the Vineyard: "I shall dig, I shall take great pains. I shall not depend on my own human efforts and energies. No, I shall strive, trusting in You, and no longer allow the graces I receive to lie sterile — graces of light, strength, interior reproaches, calls to goodness. I shall use manure, that is, I shall humble myself by learning to know myself without becoming depressed or defiant. I shall be simple and frank, calmly acknowledging the truth about myself."

O Mary intercede for me. Please say: "Let it alone this year too!"

The Life of Faith

To form an interior spirit, or to be more exact, to allow God to form it within us, we must first of all look at everything in the light of faith. The life of interior union, of docility, that is, of loving and faithful attention to God teaching us, to God training and testing us, to God present and acting within us — this life is a life of faith.

Faith in this context does not mean a passing act by which we accede to God and are justified by Him. It means the virtue of faith, the stable and infused gift that obtains its normal, supernatural effects within us. In short, we are speaking of "the supernatural habit that gives the diverse manifestations of Christian life their impulsion, their orientation, and their tonality."[1] And we are considering this virtue in ourselves, adult Christians, not in an infant whose faculties are still dormant and in whom human cooperation is reduced to an almost passive minimum.

The just man lives by faith (cf. Rom. 1:17). This formula of St. Paul's sums up his entire teaching and the entire Gospel. Without going into theology, it suffices to recall that our whole supernatural, Christian, divine life, our grace, which is a gift of God, is founded on faith. This faith is an act of the intellectual order since it consists in our intellect's adherence to God's testimony, and it is likewise a voluntary act. As St. Thomas teaches: "The will holds primacy in the act of faith."

Faith is indeed an act commanded by the will that acknowledges and loves God and hopes in Him as the First Good, the Supreme Good, the Last End, the One without whom nothing can endure, or satisfy, or beatify, the One who contains in Himself in plenitude and perfection all that we can think, desire, or will that is beautiful, right, and good.

Such being the case, let us meditate a little on the words: The just man lives by faith. What does this mean? It means that the just man lives by God through faith. God alone matters to him, God alone suffices for him.

God alone matters to him. Everything else possesses goodness only through God, and God is worth much more than His gifts. God is primordial goodness, *bonitas fontalis*. The water of a brook is good when it flows over sand: it cleanses, refreshes, it even sings in its own way. But this water comes from a spring. Cut off its source, exhaust

---

[1] F. Prat, *La Théologie de Saint Paul* (Paris: Beauchesne, 1923), Vol. II, p. 469.

the water in the spring, divert its course, dry it up, poison it, and that is the end. Instead of so many good things, there is drouth, thirst, sterility, sickness, death. So is it of every good that is cut off from its source which is God.

There is good in me. How much of this good comes from me? The Church answers:

"No one has anything of his own except falsehood and sin; if, however, man possesses any truth and righteousness, it comes to him from the wellspring for which we must all thirst, in this desert, so that refreshed by it as by drops of dew we may not fall swooning by the wayside."[2]

There is good in others, great good that attracts me and could hold me, seduce me, bind me, because in itself, in the human mode this good is proportioned to my human faculties. It is diluted, capable of being assimilated by me. What do creatures possess that is properly their own? "Falsehood and sin." The rest is the grace of God. In creatures there is goodness, but in Him it is more perfect; in them it is mixed, but in Him it is pure; in them it is finite, always corruptible and a possible agent of their own corruption, but in God it is infinite, incorruptible, and perfectly pure; in them it is variable and relatively poor, but in God it is invariable and immensely rich and diversified.

For the just man who lives by faith, *God alone suffices*. The just man knows that everything else that satisfies or tempts him, within himself or outside himself, can be found in God. For every created good that can give him selfish satisfaction or a vicarious sense of possession, everything that he holds to be good, pleasurable, sweet, the object of desire, of hope, is found in God not in a mixed, imperfect, ephemeral, exhaustible, impure state, but in a pure, perfect, inexhaustible state, infinite in its virtualities, infinite in the diversity of happiness and joy it can give, eternal.

---

[2] "Nemo habet de suo nisi mendacium et peccatum; si quid autem habet homo veritatis et iustitiae, ab illo fonte est quem debemus sitire in hac eremo ut ex eo quasi guttis quibusdam irrorati non deficiamus in via" (Council of Orange, II, Canon 22).

Knowing these things, the just man scorns all the rest, and realizes that God alone suffices. This is particularly true if he has had some glimpse of God through the infused love of contemplation, which is consciously infused faith serving as a mirror to contemplate God. The same is true of the just man who attains to some knowledge of God through a very pure love of charity. He is the man in the Gospel who, having found a precious pearl, an infinitely precious pearl, goes and sells all that he possesses to buy it, fully aware that he is driving a wonderful bargain.

Loving All Things in God

Whatever is not God must not be loved independently of Him, but in Him, for Him, and through Him.

Among all the things that are not God, I must first include myself. Nothing is more personal to me than my "self." I love nothing so much as myself, my happiness, my pleasure, my health, my reputation, my tastes, my passions, my desires, my ambitions, the animal that is in me and the quasi-angel that is in me. Sometimes by the grace of God I sense my own nothingness, my shame, my wickedness. But naturally and invincibly, I flatter myself, I caress myself, I take delight in myself. But there is also nobility and goodness in me. Of course, it does not come from me: "You are beautiful, but do not admire yourself lest you lose what you have received: admire God who has made you beautiful." Indeed, "what hast thou that thou hast not received? And if thou hast received it, why dost thou boast as if thou hadst not received it?" (1 Cor. 4:7).

There is good in me, but also evil: "de tuo, mendacium et peccatum" — falsehood and sin. All these things, which we shall meditate upon later, are not beautiful. They come from me, not from God who is perfect truth and purity. Hence, I must not love myself independently of God, for whatever in me is not from Him is in no sense lovable.

Among the things that are not God I must also include
all other creatures. These are very diverse and often very
beautiful: the distant stars, the charm of evening, lovely
songs, the pleasure of the eyes and of the mind, the beauty
of things and of sentiments. They are very diverse and
often very ugly, bitter, and shameful: all the forms of moral
evil, anger, jealousy, cruelty, lust, fear, forgetfulness of the
good, pilfering hands, enticements to sin; all the forms of
physical evil, sickness, tortures, the unending discomforts
of chronic illness, cold, hunger, hideous and repugnant
wounds, the smells of the dead, the laughter of the insane.

What lovable things, and what horrible things! Is there
a way of deciphering this enigma, of adopting a clear-cut
rule for governing and guiding the many diverse and powerful impressions constantly being produced in me?

Yes, there is: *Nothing must be loved or hated independently of God.* All created beauty is a trace, a reflection of the beauty of God. All goodness is a drop of water
from the primordial wellspring. All ugliness screams of
the absence of God's established order. It also proclaims the
emptiness, the congenital, absolute wretchedness of every
created thing that, having come from Him, tends to live of
itself, and withdraws (or rather tries to withdraw) from
Him.

In this light, in this perspective, everything becomes
a means of loving God and of serving Him: evil as well as
good, suffering no less than joy. Outside this light everything is chaos, caprice, a stumbling block; the life of faith
drops to the human, natural level, yields to the life of the
flesh which grieves, rejoices, becomes agitated, panic-
stricken. . . .

In this light, everything becomes clear. This present
life is a stopping place, not a homeland. The evil permitted
by God is a trial of faith, the raw material of love, the
fabric of fraternal charity. It will pass! Temporal goods
are also trials, snares for the unsuspecting who do not cry

out: "O Lord make haste to help me! The snare was broken, and we were delivered." These same goods bring consolation, repose, but — let us not forget — not final rest. They are merely samples, reflections, stimulants: "Seek God . . . Go higher!" "Do you seek the life of blessedness in mortal regions? It is not there. For where is the life of blessedness except in life?" (*Confess.* IV, 12).

Outside this life everything is a trap, an illusion, a danger for the mind. And this is perhaps especially true of those things that are noblest and purest, such as friendship between friends of God, even the delights of divine friendship.

Therefore, let us love ourselves and everything else in God, for Him, and through Him:

In God, for God overflows, penetrates, and quickens all things. His presence, His power, His judgment are everywhere. To see all things in Him is truth.   •

For Him, because the only absolute good that we can wish for ourselves and for all creatures is the possession of God Himself, in the measure of each one's capacity. Everything else must tend to this end. Otherwise it is nothing, less than nothing; for then it is an evil, the only real evil.

Through Him, because the only truly efficacious means of loving, serving, and possessing God is His gift, His grace, His mercy. It is therefore through Him that we hope for and expect every good, through His power, His goodness, His wisdom.

Note on Mental Prayer

At the beginning of St. Ignatius' *Exercises* we find a series of practical remarks called "Annotations," addressed quite as much to the one who is giving as to the one who is following the spiritual exercises. Among these remarks, the second has a particular right to fame. After saying

that the one who gives the exercises must not develop and
dilute the points *ad infinitum,* but rather "narrate the history . . . going through the points, however, only briefly,
and with a short explanation," St. Ignatius tells the reason
why. It is simply this: if the retreatant obtains through
his own efforts or receives from God light that will help
him to understand or savor the subject of meditation, even
if only slightly, he will derive much more fruit from it than
he would from long, tiresome explanations. "For it is not
the extent or abundance of knowledge that nourishes the
soul and satisfies it, but sensing and savoring [spiritual]
things inwardly."

This is a very necessary lesson, a warning against the
beginner's almost inevitable tendency to think that success
in his spiritual exercises consists in an abundance of ingenious and touching thoughts developed in orderly fashion
and culminating in a multitude of affections. Nothing could
be more false. This applies especially to intelligent, well-
educated persons who are inclined to think that when they
understand something they assimilate it in practice. It
also applies to very conscientious, anxious persons, inclined
to be frightened by very simple mental prayer denuded of
subject matter, prayer that is almost implicit.

It is not a "successful" meditation that matters, but the
interior savor (a savor that may scarcely be conscious)
that God gives us through the more or less active collaboration of our faculties. There may be times when we are
suffering veritable mental indigence and aridity. Even
then we can maintain our presence before God, much as
we would feed a dying fire, by a few aspirations, ejacula-
tions, vocal prayers, or by very slow spiritual reading. At
such times our will formulates a desire, a need, an almost
imperceptible taste, a determination to serve God purely,
at any price, and forever. (It matters not that this firm
resolve is buried under the debris of selfish, carnal sentiments, even of strong repugnances.) This is the precious
pearl.

Convincing Ourselves of Our Nothingness

The fundamental dispositions of the life of faith are:

1) God alone matters. 2) All that is not God may be loved (or feared or hated) only in God, for Him, and through Him, but never independently of Him. 3) We can take on this attitude of mind, we can live by this light in a permanent, habitual, serious way only if we are walking in the truth.

Truth is the foundation of the life of faith. And the truth is this: "We can do nothing by ourselves to attain the only good that ultimately matters through the habitual possession of divine light." "Non parum dicit, sed nihil. [The Lord] does not say we can do little, but nothing." (St. Augustine).

This way of looking at things, this power to put things in their right place, this salutary orientation, this adoption of the only path that leads to our eternal home, in short, this conversion, is not the fruit of our own efforts but a gift of God. It is a truth of faith:

"Anyone who affirms that he can, through his natural powers, conceive rightly any good thought for his eternal salvation, or choose it, or consent to the salutary preaching of the Gospel without the illumination and inspiration of the Holy Spirit who gives to all men sweetness in consent to and faith in divine truth, is deceived by a spirit of heresy and does not understand the words of God in the Gospel: Without me you can do nothing."[3]

In short, on this fundamental point as on all the others: "You have not chosen me, but I have chosen you, and have

---

[3] "Si quis per naturae vigorem bonum aliquid, quod ad salutem pertinet vitae aeternae, cogitare ut expedit, aut eligere, sive salutari, id est evangelicae praedicationi consentire posse confirmat absque illuminatione et inspiratione Spiritus Sancti, qui dat omnibus suavitatem in consentiendo et credendo veritati, haeretico fallitur spiritu, non intellegens vocem Dei in evangelio dicentis: sine me nihil potestis facere" (Council of Orange, II, Canon 7).

appointed you that you should go and bear fruit, and that
your fruit should remain" (John 15:16).

And St. Augustine comments admirably: "It is not I
who chose you [Lord]. And this is an ineffable grace"
(*Tract. in Joa.* 86, 2). For if I had chosen you, Lord, my
choice would have been founded on the nothingness of my
human will; whereas coming from you it has the strength
of your divine mercy, the sureness of your infallible wisdom.

I speak rightly of the nothingness and not merely of
the weakness of my human faculties with regard to the
major acts of my religious life. Of myself I am utterly
incapable of thinking correctly about salvation and about
union with God. I might think as an intelligent man, perhaps as a penetrating scholar, a philosopher, but not as a
Christian, not as a saint. Nor could I make the opportune
choices. For not even the wisest of men can, without the
help of grace, choose what is fitting, what is pleasing to
God, what is good for others and for himself, either in great
matters or small. Without the help of grace he cannot
accept God's teachings, he cannot say "Yes!" to the in-
vitations of the Holy Spirit, whether they be of a personal
or a general nature. Without grace, the other human
natural, carnal motives will retain their preponderant influence over his mind, and temptations will conquer.

But here is the antithesis, the converse fullness of this
terrible void, the remedy for this evil, the solution to this
troublesome problem: By the single fact that through my
faithfulness to God I am in a state of friendship with Him,
by the single fact that I implore His grace loyally and sincerely, I am certain of obtaining not only strength as such,
the capacity to believe, but also facility, sweetness, and
delight in believing and accepting divine truth — "suavitatem in consentiendo at credendo veritati." For the Holy
Spirit gives to all, hence to the poorest, the most wretched,
the most wicked, providing at least they want to be good.

How can this be? Through the inspiration and illumination of the Holy Spirit. This twofold power acts upon the

mind, making it see what is pleasing to God in the light of faith; and it acts upon the will (and even upon the emotions and affections which are under the dominion of the will), impelling, inspiring, and stimulating it to do good, and placing it under the happy necessity of willing and loving even what is hard and painful, providing God is thereby well served.

Domine, da mihi Spiritum bonum. . . .

Suggested Reading

Imitation of Christ, Book III, Chapter 2.

Epistle to the Hebrews, Chapter 11, Chapter 12:1-2.

Lead us, Lord, by your admirable ways, until you bring us to the principle of [spiritual] health and goodness, namely the Holy Spirit, who has made up for our sins, healed our wounds, and given the life of love to our hard hearts.
(*Spiritual Journal* of St. Francis Borgia, November 25, 1565).

Love God for God's sake, and love yourself in Him but because of Him. You truly love yourself [and you truly love your brothers] if you love God in yourself [and in them] or because He is in you [and in them] or so that He may be in you [and in them]. (St. Augustine, *Sermo* 336:2).

It is not I who chose you, Lord. And this is an ineffable grace. [That is to say, my vocation is not built on the sand of a sentiment, of a choice, of a human view of things, but on the unshakable rock of the will of God, enlightened by His wisdom, aided by His mercy.]

(St. Augustine, *Tract. 86 in Joa.* 2).

2.

The Fall and Repentance of St. Peter (Matt. 26:31-35; 40-43; 58; 69-72)

Note the preliminaries of the fall: Peter's presumption: "Even though all shall be scandalized because of thee, I will never be scandalized." His negligence and tor-

por: Peter does not watch nor pray. His curiosity: "to
see the end."

The very rapid and complete fall, brought about by two
servant girls, then by the high priest's attendants, the
denials, the oaths.

The crowing of the cock and the remembrance of Jesus'
words, accompanied by an interior grace. Peter does not
harden his heart: he is docile to God.

Immediate and exemplary repentance. He flees the
occasion of sin, turns away weeping bitterly. This great
sinner will win out over all the almost-innocents who are
not generous.

Advice on the Particular Examen

We must know ourselves, know our faults, our imper-
fections, our disordered passions, our sins. That is the
solid foundation of humility. It is the condition of serious
amendment. How can we accomplish this? In two ways.
1) We must make ourselves known to our confessor and
listen to what he tells us. For, while he is inclined to judge
what we say to him primarily on the basis of what he knows
of us, and while he is irremediably inclined to see us and
judge us in the best possible light on many points, he will
tell us many useful, in fact indispensable things if he is not
totally lacking in spiritual insight and courage. He has
the grace for this. 2) We must make ourselves known to
our superiors and listen to what they tell us. Here it is
less a question of sins than of unruly passions, disorders,
and faults, the latter including excesses as well as deficiencies.

In a sense, it is more important for our interior life
that we make ourselves known to our superiors. At the
start of our spiritual life our superiors understand what
we say to them and are inclined to judge us in the best
possible light. But they know our deficiencies, our weak
points, our small or great passions much better than our

confessors, either through others or through their own observation. They too have the grace to warn us. But it is our supernatural confidence in them (as the ordinary instruments of God in our regard) and our generosity that determine the efficacy of their efforts. It is up to us to put them at their ease, to accept their reprimands in a good spirit even when they are not asked for, even when they are unexpected, even when at first glance they appear undeserved or excessive. There is a lot of truth in the reproaches we receive. That is a basic principle. Often there is more truth than we ourselves believe, because we tend to be biased in our own regard, biased rather than indulgent in the case of those of us who are serving God as well as we can.

To make ourselves known to our confessor and to our superiors, and to judge ourselves without bias, we must first of all learn to know ourselves and hence examine ourselves. How? St. Augustine counsels nothing less to the man who wants to know himself thoroughly than to put himself to the question in the ancient sense of the word: "Now interrogate yourself, question yourself inwardly, look within yourself, consider yourself inwardly, examine yourself inwardly: sit beside yourself . . . and stretch yourself out on the rack of the commandments of God; torture yourself with fear and do not coddle yourself, but answer your own questions" (*Sermo* 107, 9).

Thus we must look within ourselves, deep, deep within. We must force ourselves to stand as defendants and stretch ourselves out in the stocks, and in this state put ourselves to the question of fear, and do it without pity.

This approach may seem a bit terrifying, and would disturb the pusillanimous rather than help them. I propose a much gentler means, which consists in imitating the woodpecker. This handsome bird grips the bark of trees with his sharp claws at those points where he thinks an insect has bored in. With his strong beak he sounds out and strikes the wood, recognizing by the sound the cavities where the stag beetles, and other boring insects are hidden. When he has discovered some of these insects, he makes an incision in the wound and crunches the insects, thus maintaining the health and sap of the tree.

We must be woodpeckers in our daily examens. These examens consist not in ruminating without end over our miseries, but in seeing quickly and clearly if we are faithful in God's service on the particular point that we want to correct (particular examen) and in our whole life (general examen). Are we docile to God?

We are Sinners

We recalled above the first condition of the life of faith, which is the deep, personal conviction of our own nothingness in all that concerns the spiritual life, the conviction of our absolute need of grace. That establishes us in the truth. It is a fundamental disposition.

It establishes us in the truth, but not in the whole truth. For not only are we incapable of doing anything good of ourselves, not only are we without capital to start this great enterprise, without liquid funds to finance this superhuman task; we are debtors, we are debilitated and sick. In short, we are sinners. We are sinners in varying degrees, but all of us are sinners without exception. And we are sinners in two respects. By reason of our sins in the strict sense of the word, and by reason of the habitual disorder of our faculties. Let us meditate upon the first of these claims. While not a very pleasant subject, it is a most useful one.

Let us note that the matter of sin is not in itself evil. Everything that God has made is good. If human beauty seduces us, leads us into temptation and sin, it is no less beautiful and good. If our own excellence intoxicates us, leads us into sinful self-satisfaction it is no less a gift of God. What is wrong is to love, as belonging to us, something that comes from God; what is wrong is to love in an excessive, selfish way something that must be loved only for the sake of God.

Such being the case, St. Augustine sets this forth as a principle: "Even though you are progressing, even though you are living a just life, you cannot live here on earth without sinning" (*Sermo* 261, 9).

And he explains that grievous sins are not the only ones, sins like theft, sacrilege, impurity, pride, and so on. There are other sins, the so-called "small" sins which no one can avoid altogether. For example:

Sins of quick enticement: "To look at what we must not look at is to sin; to listen with pleasure to what we should not listen to is to sin; to fasten our mind on an object that we should not think about is to sin" (*ibid*).

Sins of the tongue: The occasions are countless. "Lord, I am assailed each day with temptations, assailed without respite. The tongues of men are a furnace of trials for me each day. On this matter, too, you command self-mastery: give me what you command, and command what you will" (*Confessions,* 10, 29). How many sins the tongue commits! This includes every manner of evil, words that are indiscreet, words that are proud and vain, false, trifling, that is to say, useless to everyone and for any good purpose.

Sins of evil intention and sins of excess: "Most of the time when you pray your mind is elsewhere, as if you were forgetting before whom you stood, before whom you were prostrate" (*Sermo* 56, 12).

Sins of imperfect charity, of insincere forgiveness.

Although these offenses may be slight, they are sins none the less. "Do not think lightly of these sins because they are slight, but fear them because they are numerous. How small is each grain of sand! [And yet] if you put too much sand in a ship, this sand will sink it and cause its destruction" (*Sermo* 9, 17).

A grain of sand and another grain of sand, a drop of
water and another drop of water — in the end the ship
sinks, the wall crumbles. It is true that we do little at one
time, but in the end it is a great deal. This is not to say
that sins of this sort can ever accumulate to the point of
becoming a grievous sin. But they prepare the way for
serious sin, and above all they encumber and foul the
spiritual life, strain its delicate organs, impede its lofty
operations, darken the eye of the soul.

The voice of Christ: "My son, I hate thy works, and I
love thee; I hate what thou hast done, I love what I have
done."

The disciple: "O Lord, that I may not be my own life;
I have lived badly for my part, I have been my own death.
In Thee I live again" (*Sermo* 142, 4).

Advice on Spiritual Courage

Among the observations or annotations of St. Ignatius,
there is one that formulates a counsel very often repeated
in the *Exercises*. It is a counsel in which the erstwhile
army officer in him still finds expression. One might say
it is the advice to take the offensive. The best defense is
to attack:

Twelfth Annotation: He who gives the Exercises must
carefully inform the retreatant that in each Exercise he
is to persist to the end of the hour, and that he must make
an effort to be pleased at the thought that he has completed his entire hour and even done more rather than
less. . . .

More rather than less! That is the fecund principle of
the offensive. Likewise, when repugnance for real poverty
asserts itself, St. Ignatius counsels a positive appeal to God,
a plea for this poverty. When scruples strive to turn us
away from something that is unquestionably lawful, Ignatius advises to do it, and so on. This is a great principle
of the spiritual life, a principle based on a twofold founda-

tion: 1) trust in God: "He will not abandon me!"; 2) the most profound psychological observation. In a fierce battle, in a long and bitterly contested conflict, it is moral power that wins out, it is the most stubborn fighter who conquers.

Our Disordered Faculties

The truth upon which the life of faith rests is the nothingness of our own actions in spiritual matters: the nothingness of the creature, the nothingness of the sinful creature. Let us add: the nothingness of the perverse creature. For there are not only sins in the strict sense of the word, whether small or great. There is also the habitual disorder of our faculties.

I should say that for the majority of those who have begun to serve God with their whole heart, there is especially that. For the sins that they continue to commit become less frequent and diminish in gravity, are less premeditated, less deliberate, less insistent, and are committed with less acquiescence, less pleasure. They are above all acts of inadvertence, of frailty, that take them by surprise. On the other hand, many persons are not even aware of the disorder of their faculties, do not reproach themselves for it, and do not try to remedy it. And that is the greatest obstacle to the life of faith, to the life of union with God, to docility to the Holy Spirit.

Why? Because this disorder is the very root of sin, of our daily sins, whether slight or more serious. It inclines us to evil, to selfishness, to pride, to sensuality. Certainly, our faculties are not ordinarily corrupted to the point of demanding a great effort in order to be held in line or restored to God's service. Withal they are not rectified, they are not true. They are awry, and pull us toward evil, toward the lesser good. It is a cause of spiritual decline. Even more, it is an open door to disturbing temptation. We shall always have temptations, but the really dangerous ones are those that find a certain complicity within us. And

what encourages our various forms of complicity with
sin? The disorder of our faculties.

Finally, this same disorder disharmonizes the delicate
keys of our soul, and keeps them disharmonized with the
inspirations of the Holy Spirit. Thus our receptiveness to
the divine action and impulsions that are the gifts of the
Holy Spirit is lessened, our faculties are darkened, rendered obtuse and unreliable.

In what does this disorder consist? In that our faculties
for contemplation or action retain a bent, an inclination,
a deviation toward what we are not permitted to have, toward what we are not permitted to enjoy, or at least to
enjoy in certain ways. For example: a capable and influ-
ential person begins to serve God and makes great apostolic
progress. He also makes great sacrifices, leaves his family,
mortifies himself, becomes hardened to suffering, acquires
the habit of hard, patient work. But the motive behind all
this generous activity is a deep-seated and anxious desire
that is not sufficiently combatted or at least not overcome,
to judge his own actions and find satisfaction in them. That
is the disorder.

Again, the disorder may consist in a more or less subtle
vestige of sensuality that continues to govern our subcon-
scious actions. Often, very often, this tendency will be
fought, confuted by the very demands of our service or by
acts that are positively contrary to sensuality. Withal, our
sensuality remains hidden, firmly entrenched, and powerful. The proof of it is that at the first moment of inatten-
tion, weakening, or forgetfulness on our part, our sensuality
acts like a runaway horse, with immediate assurance and
competency. That is the disorder. What I am saying of
sensuality applies to sloth, gluttony, to the need for sensible
or exclusive affection, and so on.

Or perhaps we have allowed undue freedom in our judgments, criticisms, and words to dominate our life. We may
have fought this tendency doggedly by means of silence,
by the humiliating avowal of our sins, and by acts of charity.
But the ingrown tendency remains, and with disconcerting

skill brings to our lips cutting words, malicious judgments, scurrilous details, etc. That is the disorder.

Such being the state of things, how can we remedy the disorder? We must first know that it exists. But above all we must detest it. And this is not so easy, or rather it is both important and difficult and calls for a powerful grace. We must never tire of asking for this grace. The difficulty stems from the fact that the disorder is generally the excess or the consequence of a fundamental disposition within us, whether physical, intellectual, or emotional. This disposition is rooted deep within us. Hence everything that tends to oppose it, to corral it within its proper limits, to restrain it, to reduce it, appears to us as undesirable, painful, almost impossible. In fact one of the great and frequent illusions in this matter consists in unduly conferring upon these disorders a stamp of intangibility, invincibility, fatality, that discourages all efforts from the start and makes them ineffective. We say: "It is stronger than I! I shall not be able to do anything about it. I am driven to it, etc." And we say this because of a secret attachment to evil.

Finally, we must correct these disorders by mortifying the passion that serves as their nursing mother. It is here that personal effort, founded on faith and grace, is demanded of us by God. And it produces the most beautiful results, on two conditions: 1) that we act with a spirit of faith, with filial trust; 2) that we act with courage and great thoroughness. We must force these disordered faculties to fast. We must go beyond what is strictly required in each case. We must do a work of supererogation, and thereby incline the faculty in question in the opposite direction. And thus we shall succeed in redressing it.

This is the practice of all the saints, of all the friends of God, of all who want to lead a life of faith. We must resolve upon it or else renounce perfection and even the pursuit of perfection. These are the rudiments, the ABC's of holiness. It is in this that abnegation consists primarily, and without it we cannot be disciples of our Lord.

Advice on Sacrifice

Annotation 16 formulates a practical rule of primary importance, and applies the offensive strategy of St. Ignatius:

In order that the Creator and Lord may act with greater sureness in His creature, if it happens that the latter is attached and inclined to some object in a disordered way, it is very expedient that he devote all his energies to attaining the opposite extreme with relation to his disordered affection.... He must insist in his prayers and other spiritual exercises.... [so that the ultimate motive of his actions in this matter may be] the service, the honor, and the glory of His divine Majesty.

Once again, this is only one application, but a most important one of the principles of St. Ignatius. The case before us is that of disordered affection, whether the object of this affection be unsuitable, as for example if the retreatant loves a person whose affection, as he has conceived it, cannot become legitimate; or if the retreatant aspires to a position, a rank that he cannot occupy without detriment to his conscience. Or it may be a well-ordered affection with regard to its object but disordered with reference to its mode, its intensity, or to the actual conditions of its exercise. For example, the retreatant may love a person, a friend, even his own relatives with an affection that prevents him from devoting himself to his labors in peace; an affection that disturbs his spiritual life, that disorientates or partially unsettles his sensibilities the way an electric current that is too strong makes a delicate galvanometer oscillate wildly. Or perhaps the retreatant is attached to an object, a function, a possession, a habit from which he must detach himself affectively and effectively in order to allow his spiritual and apostolic life to develop. God's call then encounters a keen repugnance on the part of his temperament, his will, his carnal, sensible, affective, selfish, artistic, and independent "self."

In the two last-mentioned cases, St. Ignatius counsels a vigorous and confident offensive. We might point out that these two examples of disordered affection may apply on the one hand to repugnances against a person, a superior, an occupation, a student, and on the other hand to inordinate, disordered, excessive and apparently invincible, attraction. In either case, attack with all your strength, use all your ammunition. Pray to God to help you through His providence, even at the price of a despoilment, an uprooting, a breaking, an agony, a separation: "If thy right eye is an occasion of sin to thee, pluck it out and cast it from thee" (Matt. 5:29). Protest that you want only God. Make the sacrifice simply, honestly, even if it cannot be with enthusiasm and joy. Renew this sacrifice. Demand of yourself an absolute emotional fast in the matter of expressions of affection and of inward preoccupation — in the case of a person. In the case of an occupation that you aspire to, practice a real fast. Or if you loathe an occupation, then come to grips with it with all your might. Be ready to spend your whole life doing it, just as you would be ready never to do something you are too passionately eager to do. Say: "Whom have I in Heaven but thee? And if I am with thee, earth does not delight me. . . . the Rock of my heart and my portion, God forever" (Ps. 72:25-26). Say: "Jesus, my All!"

The World and the Spirit of God

Without God and without His grace we can accomplish nothing good spiritually. For we are creatures, sinful creatures, disordered creatures, tempted creatures.

We live in "the world," a rather equivocal term that denotes a milieu positively unfavorable to the life of faith. It is a noxious, enfeebling environment. In this sinful milieu of fallen humanity, all our deviated, disordered instincts, all the forces of evil within us find powerful stimulants and occasions of sin. That is why we must of necessity meditate upon the spirit of the world. It is a prerequisite to a thorough purification and also to the possession of the whole truth.

We are using the term "the world" in the evangelical
sense, to include all habitual ways of thinking, feeling, and
acting that are obstacles to union with God, to the service
of God. The world, therefore, is the "carnal," animal element, opposed to the spiritual and the divine. It is everything that tends to make us obtuse to calls from above and
docile to the siren calls of earth.

Our Lord Himself described the world to His Apostles
during His discourse after the Last Supper:

The Spirit of truth whom the world cannot receive, because it neither sees him nor knows him (John 14:17).

Peace I leave with you, my peace I give to you; not as the
world gives do I give to you (John 14:27).

But because you are not of the world, but I have chosen
you out of the world, therefore the world hates you (John
15:19).

. . . you shall weep and lament, but the world shall rejoice
. . . but your sorrow shall be turned into joy (John 16:20).

In the world you will have affliction. But take courage, I
have overcome the world (John 16:33).

I do not pray that thou take them out of the world, but
that thou keep them from evil. They are not of the world,
even as I am not of the world (John 17:15-16).

What are some of the negative marks of the world? It
does not receive the Spirit of God, and understands nothing
about Him. The essential need, as the world sees it, is to
shun any avoidable pain; to insist on the highest cash pay-
ment for all service rendered; to assert oneself among others
at their expense, and by all effective means without thought
of their moral value; to take and to keep as much as possible for oneself. The Spirit of God, on the other hand,
inspires dedication based on abnegation, to the point of
sacrifice; selflessness, simplicity, and modesty to the point
of complete forgetfulness of self.

From this fundamental opposition between the spirit

of the world and the Spirit of God is born a contradiction with regard to peace, rest, tranquility. The world conceives of peace and promises it in terms of abundance and the secure possession of the means of pleasure, of realized ambition and triumphant egoism. The Spirit of God promises peace in poverty of spirit (that is, in detachment), in the realized gift of self, in patience, sacrifice.

And what are some of the world's positive marks? It hates apostles, and harasses them in every possible way by seduction and persecution, by caresses and insults. In the eyes of the world, an apostle is not only a dreamer, a dupe, a dunce, but also a kill-joy, a dangerous adversary, an enemy, a censor. The world has and gives the earthy joy of immediate satisfactions, of desires fulfilled, of transient, carnal delights. The Spirit of God hates and persecutes the world, rejoicing in all that displeases the world, scorning its attractions and its sanctions. In so doing, He confers upon the faithful a deep, pure and peaceful interior joy, a joy that is incomparably superior to anything the world can offer.

What conclusions does our Lord reach for His apostles? They are not to be materially separated from the world (except in the cases of special vocations). "I do not pray that thou take them out of the world, but that thou keep them from evil" (John 17:15). And how can this be accomplished? By making them invulnerable to its assaults. The real prophylaxis against the insidious attack of the world's impure air is a sound, well-formed, and immunized temperament. Then the apostle can carry on God's works in this corruptive milieu fruitfully and without danger. The apostle will then enjoy a certain incorruptibility, a certain spiritual separation even though he is very much in the world. "Though we walk in the flesh, we do not make war according to the flesh" (2 Cor. 10:3). And Jesus says of them: "Sanctify them in the truth" (John 17:17). Consecrate my apostles in the fundamental truth, in the true order of affections and works: *God first served!*

Suggested Reading

The seven Penitential Psalms.

The Imitation of Christ, Book III, Chapter 54.

. . . the Spirit of truth whom the world cannot receive
. . . . (John 14:17). In the world you will have affliction. But
take courage, I have overcome the world (John 16:33).

Do not think lightly of these sins because they are slight,
but fear them because they are numerous. How small is each
grain of sand! [And yet] if you put too much sand in a ship,
this sand will sink it and cause its destruction (St. Augustine,
Sermo 9, 17).

Voice of Christ to the sinner: "My son, I hate thy works,
and I love thee; I hate what thou hast done, I love what I have
done" (St. Augustine, *Sermo* 142, 4).

> Do not repel me, Savior,
> From Thy sacred feet!
> Hymn for the Feast of the Holy Shroud.

3.

The Visitation (Luke 1:39-56)

Mary's apostolic zeal: instead of enjoying the presence
of Jesus within her in peace, silence, and solitary recollection, she rises and quickly makes the difficult journey over
the mountainous terrain to her cousin's home.

St. Elizabeth's exclamation: What magnificent praise
and what profound humility! Let us savor these things inwardly.

Mary's answer, the mirror of her sentiments: she acknowledges in their totality the immense graces of God
within her, including the most eminent privileges. But she
returns all honor and glory to God alone. These are the
two normal acts of a life of faith: to confess the graces of
God, and to glorify Him, to render homage to Him.

Let us sing the Magnificat quietly in our hearts.

Note on Penance

Penance is so completely a part of an apostle's life that the latter is inconceivable without the former. Penance can be practiced every day and by everyone, even and above all by the sick. There are two kinds of penance: the penance that man imposes upon himself for love of God and of souls, and the penance that God Himself inflicts through His providence. In both kinds of penance, we must distinguish the ordinary from the extraordinary.

In its ordinary degree, afflictive penance is accessible to many. A minimum of health and a little courage suffice. The calls are varied, unequal, in this as in other matters. However a certain call to penance is universal for all who are truly capable of it. In its extraordinary degree, penance that goes beyond ordinary strength is a special call made to certain apostolic souls, sometimes only temporarily and sometimes permanently. And this vocation must be tested and controlled by obedience in the very measure that ordinary penance is exceeded.

But the essential element of the penitential life is the penance that God Himself inflicts. In its ordinary degree, this penance is an everyday matter since it encompasses all the discomforts, fatigues, petty sufferings and annoyances of a human life, of a laborious life, of a rugged and relatively poor life, of an apostolic life. This ordinary penance is the more painful and meritorious for those who are weaker, less sturdy, and more temperamentally inclined to rest. Thus those who cannot practice man-made penance are the ones who have the greatest merit in accepting the penance that God sends. For in this way, if they are generous and wise, they can make up for their inability to practice penances of their own choice. In its extraordinary degree, God's penance consists in the ills, afflictions, infirmities, languors, debilities, and sufferings that attack the body and the mind with sudden violence, or gradually reduce them to a very painful and sometimes agonizing condition that may last for a very long time.

The penance that God imposes is the surest, noblest, and most meritorious. It therefore possesses spiritual value of the highest order. But it is the evangelical treasure hidden in the field. Few discover it, appreciate it, and use it to the best advantage. There are few real penitents, few friends of the Cross of Jesus. Man's natural tendency is to reject all penance, to turn his back on every cross. "For many walk, of whom I have told you often and now tell you even weeping, that they are enemies of the cross of Christ" (Phil. 3:18).

The Apostolic Call

We have examined the principal obstacles to the life of faith within us: venial sin, the disorder and malfunction of our powers of feeling and acting, the incitements and intimidations of the world. But in the face of these enemy forces, the Spirit of God has not allowed Himself to remain without a witness. Jesus, in speaking of the world, closed with these words: "But take courage, I have overcome the world" (John 16:33).

And St. John, Jesus' beloved Apostle, took up the same theme, concluding: ". . . and this is the victory that overcomes the world, our faith" (1 John 5:4). And again: "You are of God, dear children, and have overcome [Antichrist], of whom you have heard that he is coming, and now is already in the world" (1 John 4:4, 3).

Wherein lies the strength of our faith? In the conviction that God is calling us to be His apostles, that is, His collaborators and His friends. "Come, follow me, and I will make you fishers of men" (Matt. 4:19). That is the formula of the apostolic call. It contains all that is essential:

Come, follow Me — for it is I who make the choice, not you. "You have not chosen me, but I have chosen you" (John 15:16). That is why this choice is lasting, sure, and also predetermined. There is no room for invention, innovation, improvisation. The way is open. What am I saying? "I am the way."

I will make you — that is to say, I will remake you, I will reform you to my own ways, by means of trials and joys, success and humiliation, apparent inaction and back-breaking work. I will remake you by using instruments of my own choice, that my providence will prepare for you.

Fishers of men, not fishers of fish. No, your elusive prey will consist of men, of immortal, redeemed souls, aspirants to eternal life, men whom you may or may not know, whose conversion you may never witness. But in the end, if you are faithful you will catch some of them. And no one will take them from you!

That is the meaning of collaborating with Christ and being an apostle. But to be an apostle is also to become a friend of Jesus. "No longer do I call you servants. . . . But I have called you friends" (John 15:15). Naturally, we remain servants. And that is already very beautiful. It already exceeds our most ambitious dreams, when we realize we are His personal servants, constantly with Him.

But beyond that, apostles become His friends. The friends of Christ! That is saying a great deal. Who can understand it? The friends of the Word of God made flesh. The friends of the all-holy and all-pure God. The friends of Mary's Son. The friends of the One who can do all things, and who will ultimately be all in all. The friends of our Lord Jesus Christ. It is good to savor this fact. And a bit frightening, too. Jesus is saying of us: My friend the sinner, my friend the lukewarm one, my friend the lazy one, my friend the indulgent one, my friend the inconstant one, my friend the selfish one, my friend the proud one. Is such a thing fitting, is it conceivable?

His friends. And as He never forces anyone, He says to us: "Do you want to be my friend?" That is what the apostolic call means.

Note on Discretion

The Eighteenth Annotation of St. Ignatius is very long but easy to summarize: to treat each one according to his

strength, not to ask more of him than he can peacefully
carry in the Lord, not to insist on lofty spirituality if he
is not capable of more than virtuous mediocrity. Let us
note that while spiritual capacity is founded on a certain
receptivity of mind, and even more on right judgment and
common sense, it is in no way determined by the extent of
one's natural talents and mental capacities. Persons of
superior intelligence obviously have advantages, but they
must pay the price of these advantages. The same is true
of persons well endowed for the arts and for the life of
affection. The thing to note here is the principle of discretion, of correct application, and the warning against a
spirit of fantasy, excessive uniformity, and ambition.

The director of the Exercises is thus invited to adapt
his lessons, counsels, and teachings to the real capacities
and powers of the retreatant, and even then not to exhaust
and overburden him beyond what he can carry peacefully
in the Lord. Now, this is a rule of conduct that we must
gradually learn to apply to ourselves. Since it is much
harder for us to do this ourselves, we must for a while depend heavily on the help provided us by spiritual direction
and obedience.

At the same time, this taste for being controlled and
directed, this prompt docility must not degenerate into
passivity. That would be too easy. Little by little we must
become accustomed to conducting ourselves in the details
of our life according to the rules that experience and authority have set down for us in support of God's call.

The principle of "peaceful effort" will be invaluable to
us. In most cases with a little recollection, perspicacity,
and wisdom on our part, it will become evident to us that
many efforts, excellent in themselves and consistent with
our vocation, can be accomplished peacefully. It will become equally clear to us that certain other efforts cannot
be so accomplished. Between the two types of effort there
will be a contested zone, in which we shall need greater
light from God, as well as advice from others. In order to

judge the right effort to make in this disputed zone we shall have to search, to make careful experiments, notably in the matter of health, effective poverty, working facilities, and so on. But the rule of St. Ignatius will very often suffice: God does not ask anything that is not feasible peacefully, that is to say, without anxiety or excessive fatigue that might have lasting, depressing effects on us.

Can You Drink My Cup?

The apostolic call is determined by the goal to be attained. And this goal is effective and total participation, as men, in the work of the Redemption: "Come, follow me, and I will make you fishers of men" (Matt. 4:19). Jesus Christ has deigned to add an incomparable complement of affection to this call, inviting those who accept the apostolic vocation to be His friends. "No longer do I call you servants. . . . But I have called you friends" (John 15:15). But everything has not yet been said. Before we answer the call with the words: "Lo, here am I. Send me" (Is. 6:8), we must understand and carefully weigh the essential condition of this call.

This condition is that the apostle be conformed to his Master, configured to his Model. His destiny must resemble the destiny of his divine Friend. It has been expressed in a thousand ways in the Gospel: "No disciple is above his teacher, nor is the servant above his master" (Matt. 10:24). The disciple must be ready to be treated like his Master. "As the Father has sent me, I also send you" (John 20:21).

Of all these formulas, let us choose for consideration one that seems to include everything, the one that Jesus used in speaking to James and John: "Can you drink of the cup of which I am about to drink?" (Matt. 20:22). That is: "Can you, with my grace — which always comes with the call and will never fail you unless you first fail it — can you follow in my footsteps? Can you imitate my life, can you be content with my portion, can you make my

tastes your own? In short, can you drink the cup that my
Father has prepared for me?

I am not asking you to find it always sweet and pleasing, inebriating and delicious. Sometimes, yes. You will
say: "My cup overflows!" (Ps. 22:5). You will put it to
your lips with delight, as I have done. But at one hour or
another, you will be forced to say with me: "Remove this
cup from me!" (Mark 14:36).

And so, O my son, O my Apostle, O my friend, can you
drink this cup as my Father has prepared it for me, as I
myself shall prepare it for you, sparing your weakness and
even taking your tastes into account in a certain sense, but
into which I shall pour the necessary gall of bitterness and
the strong liquor that bears the taste of my own cup? Can
you drink it?

I do not ask of you an enthusiastic or prophetic answer.
I know you are weak, mediocre, unstable, variable, impres-
sionable, scarcely more than a child, and sometimes less
than a child. I know that you are still passionate, capricious,
selfish, curious, irresolute. I know that you are sand to
build with, clay for the potter, mud in some of your deepest
recesses, in short, nothingness. I know that of yourself
you have only "evil and lies." But my grace is strong,
powerful, infallible in the service of my wisdom. And besides it is not you who are choosing me, it is I who am
choosing you (ineffable grace!).

Then too, I have prepared relays for you, stopping
places, aids, occasions for abnegation to your measure,
favorable circumstances demanding detachment, resignation, humility; defeats and small victories, consolations in
a visibly blessed apostolate, and dark nights to test your
faith. I have prepared for you brothers, friends, a Mother,
joys and sacrifices, everything you need to resemble me!

Well now, we have honestly debated these conditions
between us, as between honest merchants, as between Power
and power. See how I respect your fragile liberty and your

accountability! Under these conditions, under this contract of service and pledge of friendship, do you want me? Will you be able to drink my cup? Can you drink it now? "Can you drink of the cup of which I am about to drink?" (Matt. 20:22).

John and James answered: "We can!" Let us see what we should answer.

Note on Abnegation

What we have said about St. Ignatius' rule "suaviter posse ferre in Domino" (to ask no more of anyone than he can peacefully carry in the Lord) must not become a principle of reduced effort, of laziness, or cowardice. This rule concerns above all those who guide others, and it is a rule of discretion. It must be complemented, for our personal apostolic use, by an observation formulated by St. Ignatius at the end of his elaboration on the reform of our life which closes the second week of the Exercises. Here it is: "Let each one convince himself that he will make more progress in all spiritual things in the measure that he practices greater abnegation of his self-love, of his own will, of his own interest."

This is a golden maxim, the echo of the Gospel and a summing up of all ascesis. Notice the turn of the sentence. It is general advice. It is up to each one to profit by it: "more . . . in the measure that. . . ." That is the exact measure of spiritual progress in all things. If there is little abnegation, then there is little progress. If there is much abnegation, there is much progress.

Abnegation of what? Abnegation of our self-love, notably by means of simplicity, absence of self-concern, absence of egoistic self-satisfaction. Abnegation of our own will, notably by obedience, docility to God and to His authentic representatives. Abnegation of our own interest, notably by effective and affective disinterestedness. "Freely you have received, freely give" (Matt. 10:8).

"I am thy servant"

In answer to the call of Christ our Lord, we have reflected. We are called to be apostles, to live a life of friendship with the Master, to conform our life to His, up to and
including the sharing of His chalice.

What shall we answer? I suggest this answer to you:
"O Lord, I am thy servant, I am thy servant, the son of
thy handmaid" (Ps. 115:7).

O Lord: This act of faith and trust is at the beginning
of all personal, wholehearted, difficult service. "My Lord
and my God!" These were the words of St. Thomas the
Apostle after he had put his finger into the holes made by
the nails, and his hand into the pierced side of his Master.
From now on, we belong to Him in life and in death.

I am thy servant: I who am so evil, still so shackled to
my old habits, so entangled in the brambles of my selfishness, so destitute of spiritual riches, so full of wiles and
tricks to push myself forward — I am your servant. Servant, that is my definition. "I am thy servant." I repeat
it, I hold fast to it. You deign to call me your friend. That
is your affair, Lord. As for me, I keep to my place. I am
a servant. A servant is someone who does not choose his
service, who does not haggle, who does not discuss: "For
I . . . have soldiers subject to me; and I say to one, 'Go,'
and he goes; and to another, 'Come,' and he comes; and to
my servant, 'Do this,' and he does it" (Matt. 8:9).

Obviously all forms of service do not appeal to me
equally. I hope for the grace of being indifferent about the
kind of service demanded of me, but I do not count too
much on obtaining this favor. But among all services there
is one that I love, that I choose, that I embrace as my lot,
my portion. That is commanded service. It is my service
because it is yours. I am your servant. That is my joy, my
security. Your servant: I do not serve myself, I do not
serve men. Strictly speaking, I serve neither my superiors,
my equals, nor my subordinates. I serve you, Lord. It is

you that I see in them, in accordance with your words: "He who hears you, hears me" (Luke 10:16); "as long as you did it for one of these, the least of my brethren, you did it for me" (Matt. 25:40).

And the son of thy handmaid. Here is another title to glory, another source of trust. Servant, yes. But after all, I am also the son of your Servant. For you had one Servant on earth who said she was and was in fact your Servant *par excellence,* one who said in the name of all who had come before and of all who would come afterward: "Behold the handmaid of the Lord" (Luke 1:38).

This handmaid was so pleasing to you and served you so well that you entrusted yourself to her with truly filial abandon, simplicity, and plenitude, as a son entrusts himself to his mother. She was so pleasing to you that everyone who bears her colors, everyone who claims relationship to her, everyone who follows her example, pleases you also. For every son delights in the work, the influence of his mother.

Well, this handmaid is my Mother! I am your servant, but I am also the son of your handmaid. And the patronage of my Mother makes my apostolic call, as well as my thin, paltry "Yes" in answer to it, pleasing to you. It also fills my soul with a sweetness, a peace, and a security that I would never dare hope for through my own efforts. In days of trial — and alas! in days of sin — I have my sure recourse, my invincible hope. I cling to my Mother, and I have no fear lest you say to me as you once did to Abraham: "Cast out this bondwoman, and her son" (Gen. 21:10). For you will never repulse your Mother.

Suggested Reading

Imitation of Christ, Book II, Chapters 7 and 8.

Epistle to the Philippians, Chapter 1, Chapter 2:1-20.

Christ says to you: I am the way, the truth, and the life. You want to go forward? I am the way. You do not want to

err? I am the truth. You do not want to die? I am the life.
You have nowhere to go except to Me. You have no means of
going anywhere except through Me (St. Augustine, *Tract. 22 in
Joa.* 8).

Strip off the old man with his deeds, and put on the new,
one that is being renewed unto perfect knowledge "according
to the image of his Creator." Here there is not "Gentile and
Jew," "circumcised and uncircumcised," "Barbarian and
Scythian," "slave and freeman"; but Christ is all things and
in all.

Put on therefore, as God's chosen ones, holy and beloved,
a heart of mercy, kindness, humility, meekness, patience [as
though they were wedding garments]. Bear with one another
and forgive one another, . . . even as the Lord has forgiven
you, so also do you forgive. But above all these things have
charity, which is the bond of perfection. And may the peace of
Christ reign in your hearts; unto that peace, indeed, you were
called in one body. Show yourselves thankful (Col. 3:9-15).

4.

Meditations on Two Beatitudes, following St. Augustine

Blessed are the poor in spirit!

O poverty of my Lord — O poverty!
He is born in a tiny nook,
wrapped in swaddling clothes, and laid in a manger.

And then this Lord of heaven and earth, this Creator of the
angels:

sucks His Mother's breast,
cries,
feeds,
grows,
goes through the vicissitudes of growing up,
hides His majesty.

And later on He is:

seized,
scorned,

scourged,
mocked,
spit upon,
buffeted,
crowned with thorns,
hanged on a gibbet,
pierced with a lance.
O Poverty!

O Lord, when I consider your poverty, whichever way I turn, acquired riches seem vile to me . . . (St. Augustine, *Sermo* 14, 9).

Blessed are the clean of heart!

Your whole task on earth consists in healing the eye of your heart so that you may see God.

It is to this end that the most sacred Mysteries, the preaching of the word of God, and the exhortations of Holy Mother Church are ordered. And they provide you the means of correcting your habits, of bridling your carnal desires, of renouncing the world and its pomps not only in words but in fact by a sincere change of life.

Whatever
your acts,
your good deeds,
your efforts,
the calls you receive to goodness,
your laudable desires,

if you succeed in seeing God, you will not ask for anything more. What more can you seek, if God is there?

Who could satisfy you if God does not suffice!

You want to see God, you strive to see God, you burn to see God.

Reflect on what has been written: Blessed are the clean of heart, for they shall see God!

Therefore prepare the instrument to see Him. Purify your heart (St. Augustine, *Sermo* 88).

Bethlehem

The apostle's life of faith develops under the action of a divine Artist, the Holy Spirit. He is the only Artist, but His works of art are infinitely varied: "Now there are varieties of gifts, but the same Spirit. . . . To one through the Spirit is given the utterance of wisdom; and to another the utterance of knowledge, according to the same Spirit. . . . But all these things are the work of one and the same Spirit, who allots to everyone according as he will" (1 Cor. 12:4, 8, 11).

Upon this diversity, this beautiful variety, the divine Artist places His generally recognizable mark. He has His preferred features, His prototypes. It is much the way great artists have their favorite procedures, their secrets, the inimitable and profoundly personal "something" that enables us to distinguish, the instant we hear it, a theme of Beethoven, a Racine couplet, a thought of Pascal's. It is the Holy Spirit who obtains unity amid diversity in the spiritual life by offering to all who are docile to His inspirations the one perfect Exemplar, Jesus Christ, and also, secondarily, His Mother. Only imitation of Jesus can please God, only resemblance to Him can make the human soul reflect the divine.

Each friend of God, each apostle who faithfully strives to understand and imitate Jesus and Mary, receives a special resemblance to them. And so amid a great diversity of endowments and orientations the heavenly resemblances appear and become firmly impressed on each soul.

Everything in the life and teachings of Christ and of His Mother can serve as food for the life of faith, for the interior life, for the apostolic life. But there are certain cycles in their lives that are particularly inspiring and capable of bringing forth the desired likeness. These include above all the cycle of the divine Childhood and the cycle of the Passion. They are the best known in some of their details, the most accessible, the most stirring, the most universal. Let us examine a few of the episodes of the cycle of the divine Childhood.

Now it came to pass in those days, that a decree went forth from Caesar Augustus that a census of the whole world should be taken. This first census took place while Cyrinus was governor of Syria. And all were going, each to his own town, to register.

And Joseph also went from Galilee out of the town of Nazareth into Judea to the town of David, which is called Bethlehem — because he was of the house and family of David — to register, together with Mary his espoused wife, who was with child. And it came to pass while they were there, that the days for her to be delivered were fulfilled. And she brought forth her firstborn son, and wrapped him in swaddling clothes, and laid him in a manger, because there was no room for them in the inn.

And there were shepherds in the same district living in the fields and keeping watch over their flock by night. And behold, an angel of the Lord stood by them and the glory of God shone round about them, and they feared exceedingly (Luke 2:1-9).

This text brings to life before our eyes the great commotion caused by the Roman decree for a world-wide census. Everybody started moving. And Joseph also set out from Nazareth for Bethlehem, the town of his forbears, in order to register. But in God's plans, all these far-flung movements of people were simply ordained so that the Child might be born in Bethlehem in great poverty. In our own times, we can also discover a divine purpose in the great movements of men all over the world, and in the course of national and international affairs during the twentieth century. God's wisdom still rules: "She reacheth therefore from end to end mightily, and ordereth all things sweetly" (Wisd. 8:1).

Mary's sentiments before the birth of Jesus were divided. She was glad to have Jesus remain hidden within her, not because of the joy it gave her (for Mary never allowed the thought of her personal joy to influence her), but because He was thus sheltered from the wicked, from the importunate, from personages of importance. If He were to appear, if He came into the world, He would be exposed to every danger, and even she could do little to defend Him from evil, from attack. And yet this was inherent in His role as Savior. This is why He had come. Therefore: "Come, Lord, do not delay!"

Let us unite ourselves to the shepherds to whom a great joy was announced for themselves and for all the people "for today . . . a Savior has been born to you, who is Christ the Lord. And this shall be a sign to you: you will find an infant wrapped in swaddling clothes and lying in a manger" (Luke 2:11-12).

Note on Scruples

Let us now pass from St. Ignatius' Annotations to several less known rules for recognizing and distinguishing scruples, and hence for correcting and eliminating them. May our Lord and God preserve us from scruples!

St. Ignatius first distinguishes scruples in the strict sense from false judgment which sees a sin where there is none. A scruple, as he sees it, is an anxious state of doubt suggested from without regarding the moral value of an act already performed or still to be performed, and causing uncertainty and confusion. False judgments are altogether bad, because they are nothing but error. They should therefore be corrected. Scruples on the other hand can and often do have some spiritual usefulness, at least for a while. In producing a temporary and surmountable crisis they refine a conscience that lacks delicacy and awaken the soul violently to every semblance of moral evil.

St. Ignatius points out that the devil makes use of scruples or their opposite (i.e., moral laxism), according to each one's temperament, antecedents, and inclinations. To those who are lax he suggests an ever greater laxity. "It is not a great sin. It is a very small matter, it is an imperfection. Is it even a sin at all?" To the cowardly, the inwardly divided, the undecided, he suggests an ever greater stringency of conscience. "That is wrong, very wrong. I have certainly sinned, although I do not know exactly in what respect. . . . I had better not practice penance. It might upset me. I had better not push myself forward and do this task. It would incite me to vanity. Or else I would spoil everything." And so on.

What to do in the face of these snares? We should fight back and outmaneuver the devil's tactics. Thus we shall gradually attain an approach based on solid common sense and on the peaceful middle ground which is the condition of all fruitful work and spiritual progress. And how shall we do it? Through obedience and severity in the case of suggested laxism. Through indulgence in the case of suggested scruples and anxiety. For instance, we may be inwardly inspired to do something good that is quite traditional and accepted in the Church of God. If contrariwise a disturbing, piercing thought comes to us from the outside that we should not do it, that it would expose us to vainglory, and so on, then we must raise up our mind to God and, if there is nothing in the act contrary to the service of God, act boldly, cut through vain fears, and say to the devil: "I did not begin for your sake, and I shall not stop for your sake" (St. Bernard).

The Flight into Egypt

After the Magi had departed, an angel warned Joseph during his sleep and said to him:

"Arise, and take the child and his mother, and flee into Egypt, and remain there until I tell thee. For Herod will seek the child to destroy him." So he arose, and took the child and his mother by night, and withdrew into Egypt, and remained there until the death of Herod (Matt. 2:13-15).

What a magnificent example of obedience! The angel commands clearly, firmly, offering no possibility of refusal. He gives reasons for the period of exile and trial, but leaves its duration indefinite. Joseph arises in the dead of night; and notwithstanding their weariness, the need of awakening the child with a start, and the haste needed to pack up their poor belongings, they set out.

Need we say that God could have arranged things differently, saved His Son in some other way, and foiled the plans of the terrible tyrant? But He did nothing of the sort. Instead, He allowed second causes, men's freedom to persecute, to follow their course even to and including the martyrdom of the Holy Innocents. He also saved what needed to be saved by means of great discomforts on an improvised journey and by means of an indefinite sojourn in an unknown and perhaps hostile land.

Mary's sentiments amid all these happenings: she accepts as quite natural the fact that she was not the first to be warned but had to be told by Joseph, that she has been disturbed and sent off like a package. She is very much afraid for her child's welfare, and feels that as long as she is with Him there can be no exile for her. Her first concern is to protect Him; nothing else matters. She adores the will of God with serenity in the face of this hurried departure and sudden fear: "The Lord is my shepherd: I want for nothing" (Ps. 22:1).

To Joseph she says: "Everything will be all right. God is protecting us and He will protect the child." She says only a few brief words, and wastes no time prattling. She does not say: "What a misfortune! What a bother!" and so on. She carries the child away with great care. For, pressed for time or not, she must do everything as well as possible. Then she abandons herself to God's care.

And Jesus Advanced in Wisdom

And the child grew and became strong. He was full of wisdom and the grace of God was upon him . . . . And Jesus advanced in wisdom and age and grace before God and men (Luke 2:40, 52).

During the long period stretching from the return from Egypt to the public life (except for the episode in the Temple), the Evangelist stresses three aspects of Jesus' progress, whether real or apparent:

Physical progress: "And the child grew, gained strength, increased in size." That is the most probable meaning of the word ἡλιχία in Verse 52. The fact is that physical strength, health, are of great importance in the life of faith, in the spiritual and apostolic life. On this point St. Ignatius says very well: "A moderate care to conserve [and let us add: increase] one's bodily strength so that it may be used in the service of God is worthy of praise, and everyone must have such care."

Progress in wisdom. This progress was apparent, for all the treasures of the knowledge and wisdom of God were in Him from the beginning. We have been stressing "wisdom" as one of the most desirable traits of an apostle. This beautiful word covers diverse qualities and a general attitude on life which consists in not being uselessly impassioned in our actions. It involves the curbing of all carnal, selfish, impure passions; that is, passions disordered in their object or in their mode, futile passions, and finally all passions that are useless either to the spiritual good of the one who experiences or communicates them, or to the spiritual good of others. There are noble, holy passions that we must feed and accept (while controlling them for fear of excesses and the forming of dangerous habits), passions that we must kindle. Such are the apostolic passion, the passion of love of God, of our Lord Jesus Christ, of fraternal self-sacrifice. Among these also are the passion for work, for exerting a wholesome influence upon others, but these must be encouraged only up to a certain point. There are also passions that have selfish or disturbing repercussions, and these we must tame, extenuate by means of an emotional fast, mortify by prayer, and sacrifice

out of love of God. This is one of the hardest, most necessary, and most laborious tasks of our life of faith. Let us
pray, therefore.

Spiritual progress: "The grace of God was upon him.
. . . Jesus advanced in . . . grace." This was apparent
progress. The heart of apostolic action consists in making
others sense distinctly or indistinctly that grace is upon us.
And to achieve this end, grace must in fact be upon us, and
not merely in the degree known as the theological "state
of grace." It must be in us in abundance, and increasingly
so. Nothing can make up for a lack of grace on our part.
On the contrary, this grace is divine life itself. We must
therefore ask for grace, nurture it within us by all means,
and place it above everything else in our esteem and love.
We must also strive to obtain it through abnegation, according to the recommendation of St. Ignatius.

Suggested Reading

The Gospel according to St. Luke, Chapter 2.

The Imitation of Christ, Book III, Chapters 5 and 6.

Oh, Holy Spirit, come into my heart.
Draw it by Thy power to Thee, true God,
Grant me love with fear of Thee.
Guard me from all evil thought,
Warm me and inflame me with Thy love,
Holy my Father and sweet my Lord,
Help me now in all my labors.
Christ who art Love, Christ who art Love
                    (Prayer of St. Catherine of Siena).[1]

And this shall be a sign to you: you will find an infant
wrapped in swaddling clothes and lying in a manger (Luke
2:12).

Let each one convince himself that he will make more
progress in all spiritual things in the measure that he practices
greater abnegation of his self-love, of his own will, and of his
own interest. (St. Ignatius, *De emendatione vitae,* conclusion.)

---

[1] Johannes Jørgensen, *Saint Catherine of Siena* (London: Longmans,
Green & Co., 1939), p. 272.

My yoke, says Christ, is not a burden that bears down on a heavily-laden man, but the wings of one who would fly. Birds carry the burden of their wings; they carry them and in turn are borne up by them. They carry their wings on the earth, and their wings bear them up in the sky (St. Augustine, *Sermo* 164, 7).

5.

Meditation on a Few of Our Lord's Last Words (John 17)

"Now this is everlasting life, that they may know thee, the only true God, and him whom thou hast sent, Jesus Christ" (John 17:3).

Our life will be spent striving to obtain this everlasting life.

"I pray for them [my disciples] . . . . Holy Father, keep in thy name those whom thou hast given me, that they may be one even as we are" (John 17:9, 11).

Keep us, Lord. We would not know how to keep ourselves. Unite us, Lord, unite us in you, for your glory, for our strength, for our joy.

"I do not pray that thou take them out of the world, but that thou keep them from evil [from sin]" (John 17: 15).

"Yet not for these only do I pray, but for those also who through their word are to believe in me" (John 17:20).

"[Father], that the love with which thou hast loved me may be in them, and I in them" (John 17:26).

Note on Election

The high point in the *Exercises* of St. Ignatius is the election of a state of life. The hypothesis is that the retreatant is a man called by God to a life of faith, a serious apostolic life, in a degree that is still unknown. Should he remain in the world? Should he enter Orders? Should he become a religious? By hypothesis the man is still free to choose his destiny. But it goes without saying that the essential aspects of election continue to apply for those who are no longer free to choose because they are already in a normally definitive state, having already chosen or engaged themselves by an equivalent, implicit choice. How, then, can election apply to them? Actually the spirit of election retains all its meaning for them.

And this spirit consists in the orientation of one's life, not according to carnal, human, natural attractions, repugnances, and passions, but according to the views of God, honestly sought and peacefully accepted in their totality. All the reality of the spirit of election subsists in everything that concerns the practice of the dedicated life, although the fundamental choice has already been made. The general choice is beautiful, indispensable, decisive in a sense, but it does not suffice. This choice determines the road to be followed, but it does not set our feet upon it. We must still go forward, remain faithful, overcome obstacles, level off the rough spots, and finally enlist others in the path that is best for them.

To this end, resolutions will prove useful. These resolutions may be short or long, one or many, general or specific, according to the needs, tastes, and inclinations of each one. Whichever way we go about it, we must always try to determine, to pinpoint our dominant and disordered passion, or the network of such passions. This we can do with the help of God by means of backward glances over our past life, by a keener awareness that God will give us of our deficiencies or of our vocation, and by counsel wisely sought.

We may be faced with an evil or dangerous tendency, or simply a tendency to excess, a tendency to egoism. Perhaps we tend to make ourselves the center of our universe, to speak too much about ourselves, think too much about ourselves, to be too self-satisfied. We may tend to compare ourselves too much with others, to become too easily discouraged, to worry. We may be afraid of doing too much for God. We may act and think as if our spiritual powerhouse were within us instead of in God. Conversely, our problem may relate to altruism. We may have too strong, too natural, and insufficiently mortified affection, affection that is too encumbering, engrossing, and perhaps paralyzing, for one or more persons, one or more types of work, a particular place, and so on. Or we may have uncontrolled aversion for certain persons, occupations, places, and so on.

Once we have made this inventory, whether in writing or not, as clearly as possible and with God's light, we must also implore this light through the intercession of the Blessed Virgin. Then we shall see clearly the reform that is possible, desirable, requested of us by God, and which we can carry through peacefully. Each one must formulate the goals of this reform, and the practical means of attaining them. These means will include advice from qualified persons, self-examination, sanctions, the giving of accounts, and so on. Finally, we must strive to discover and keep in mind a few stimulants, a few words filled with spiritual meaning that can nourish us, inspire us, and console us; the remembrance of God's mercy and His Mother's toward us, the remembrance of graces received that will reassure and pacify us, and make us better, happier.

The Bonds of Jesus

Now that we have meditated upon a few episodes in the cycle of the divine Childhood, we shall next fix our eyes and hearts upon the cycle of the Cross and Passion of Christ. There is nothing better. "God forbid that I should glory save in the cross of our Lord Jesus Christ, through whom the world is crucified to me, and I to the world" (Gal. 6:14). That means that the Cross of Christ, His gibbet, a mark of infamy and an instrument of torture, has become for St. Paul and for every true Christian a sign of honor. It has become an acceptable, desirable, delectable perspective. And hence "the world," the carnal element, which is the enemy of the Spirit and of the life of faith, is thereby "crucified," becomes an object of horror and scorn for Paul and for every true Christian, and vice versa.

Then they came forward and set hands on Jesus and took him [to Gethsemani]. . . . Now those who had taken Jesus led him away to Caiphas the high priest . . . . And they bound him and led him away, and delivered him to Pontius Pilate the procurator (Matt. 26:50, 57; 27:2). And the men who had him in custody began to mock him and beat him (Luke 22:63).

It is humiliating and painful to be bound by men. Humiliating, because it is a constraint unworthy of a free and reasonable man; painful, because we are thus rendered helpless, delivered up to the arbitrary will of anyone who would outrage us.

It is noble to be bound by the Holy Spirit: "And now, behold, I am . . . compelled [bound] by the Spirit" (Acts 20:22). For these bonds are altogether beneficial. They fasten us to what is good, making our life depend on the only Master who has absolute power over it, and emancipating us from all evil and lowly servitudes. Besides, we accept these bonds voluntarily and renounce only carnal, sinful independence.

The bonds of Jesus are humiliating and painful. Ours are holy and sweet, and unite us to Him. If our bonds sometimes weigh heavily upon us, let us think of His.

Mary saw her Son bound, dragged, at the mercy of brutal and hateful people.

The Crucifixion

Then the soldiers of the procurator took Jesus [after the scourging] into the praetorium, and gathered together about him the whole cohort. And they stripped him [of his garments stuck to his wounds] and put on him a scarlet [soldier's] cloak; and plaiting a crown of thorns, they put it upon his head, and a reed into his right hand [in lieu of a scepter]; and bending the knee before him they mocked him, saying, "Hail, King of the Jews!" And they spat on him, and took the reed and kept striking him on the head (Matt. 27:27-30).

Jesus' attire is painful and derisory. The crown is plaited with sharp and penetrating thorns.

Jesus' scepter is powerless to inspire fear or respect, but very well suited to make Him suffer in His flesh and in His honor.

The homage rendered to Jesus is mockery, accompanied by gross insults.

That is why "they who belong to Christ have crucified their flesh [their carnal pride, everything that is an obstacle to divine inspirations, to the Holy Spirit] with its passions and desires" (Gal. 5:24).

The soldiers therefore, when they had crucified him, took his garments and made of them four parts, to each soldier a part, and also the tunic. Now the tunic was without seam, woven in one piece from the top. They therefore said to one another, "Let us not tear it, but let us cast lots for it, to see whose it shall be" .... These things therefore the soldiers did.

Now there were standing by the cross of Jesus his mother and his mother's sister, Mary of Cleophas, and Mary Magdalene. When Jesus, therefore, saw his mother and the disciple standing by, whom he loved, he said to his mother, "Woman, behold, thy son." Then he said to the disciple, "Behold, thy mother." And from that hour the disciple took her into his home (John 19:23-27).

Jesus' garments: the trifling and cruelly commonplace circumstances of life. The dividing up before the eyes of Mary! And the seamless tunic — what a precious relic is being snatched from her!

Jesus' friends are standing. The company of the friends of the Cross is a small one. Jesus has few friends who love Him even when He is hanging on the Cross. He has the faithful friendship of Mary Salome, the penitent, burning love of Mary Magdalene, and of course John and Mary are there.

Mary's sentiments are very simple. She is suffering absolutely, to the utmost limit that any creature is capable of suffering, and she resigns herself absolutely. "Shall I not drink the cup that the Father has given me?" (John 18:11). Let us not try to console her. Let us remain at her feet, with respect, fear, and silence.

Jesus' legacy: Alas! What a son He bequeathes in His place! But He has to assure Mary of shelter, support, a home. Mary's answer is not recorded. She probably says nothing. A look, an interior assent, an acceptance without condition or thought of herself. John answers with immediate, unlimited, filial devotion. "From that hour. . . ."

Suggested Reading

The Imitation of Christ, Book III, Chapters 40 and 42.

The Passion, according to St. John, Chapters 18 and 19.

God forbid that I should glory save in the cross of our Lord Jesus Christ, through whom the world is crucified [that is to say, is an object of horror, fear, and scorn] to me, and I to the world (Gal. 6:14).

For many walk, of whom I have told you often and now tell you even weeping, that they are enemies of the cross of Christ (Phil. 3:18).

But Mary kept in mind all these things, pondering them in her heart (Luke 2:19).

VIII

ON THE PURIFICATION
OF THE APOSTLE

1.

I am the Lord

The general prerequisite for any serious reform, as for
any correct spiritual election, is the renewal within us of
the fundamental truth of religion. All sincere religion
"in spirit and in truth" is a conversation, a filial exchange
between man and his God. The essential condition for this
conversation, this divine friendship, is to know with some
exactitude who God is and what man is. The whole of our
religion, of our relations with God must in fact be founded
on and governed by this knowledge.

It is always important to renew within us this knowledge that we already possess, and to make every effort to
deepen it. We must do this without contention, peacefully,
but with our whole mind and our whole strength.

Especially with our whole mind. It is first of all a
meditation, that is, a series of reflections intended to increase the light within us. And St. Ignatius proposes it to
us in the form of a mental exercise, without indicating any
preliminary prayers or preludes to help the imagination
and the emotions. In short, it is mental prayer to be
accomplished while sitting down. Certain types of mental

167

prayer demand that we stand up, such as the prayer of the
Kingdom; others require us to lie prostrate, like the prayer
of the *Three Degrees of Humility.* Still others, like the
one on *Sin,* call for a kneeling position.

We have the right to take advantage of the light of
Revelation during our meditation. It is quite unnecessary
to place ourselves by a sort of methodical doubt, of methodical abstention, in the state of mind of the good pagan! That
would be a useless regression, even if it were really possible.

Who are you, Lord, and who am I? You are the Lord:
"I am the Lord your God" (Lev. 18:2). You are subsistent
Love: "God is love" (I John 4:16).

You are the Lord. A man will say: "This harvest is
mine," because he has toiled, sowed, hoed, and reaped on
a piece of rented land. He says it with a better right when
the soil has been bequeathed him by his father and his
father's father. Then the land with its buildings and
appurtenances are his in a certain sense. This is not a
temporary right. It is an enduring right that he can assert.
He is the owner. It is a great honor to own a field. Withal
this right remains precarious, because the man who owns
and cultivates this field did not create it. He merely
occupies it. He did not fashion the soil from nothing, make
it habitable, arable, by a beneficent ordering of climate and
sunlight.

God is the Lord because He not only occupies the field
that I am, He possesses it, topsoil and subsoil, *He made it.*
Without Him, nothing would exist. Neither the harvest, nor
the soil. Everything comes from Him, everything belongs
to Him: *I am the Lord.*

This right of God's is essential, inalienable. It is written
into the very texture of my being, like names woven into
a fabric by the disposition of the threads that compose it.
Wherever a yard of this cloth is held up to the light, it
cries out the name of the One who made it: *I am the Lord.*

This right of God's is incommunicable. Every legitimate right over me is an emanation, a delegation of His right. Every just submission relates to His authority, every form of dominion exists only as subordinate to His kingship, and must in the end relate to it (cf. John 19:11).

This right of God's is total. If I withdraw a single fiber of my heart from it, a single thought of my mind, a flash of my intellect, or movement of my body; if I consciously and deliberately withdraw from it the least of my acts, I am guilty of pillage, injustice, robbery, indelicacy. And I am also guilty of error, stupidity. I have been tricked. "They who go far from thee, shall perish, thou destroyest all who are disloyal to thee" (Ps. 72:27). It is an error, it is one of those savage efforts condemned in advance, which escapes the Providence of grace and predilection only to fall under the Providence of justice and wrath: "Who is like unto God?" *I am the Lord.*

This right of God's is eternal. Heaven and earth will pass. Human pleasure and pain will pass. Laughter and tears will pass. The arts and books will pass. Affection and devotion will pass. Faith and hope will pass. But the dominion of God and its consequences over me, whether for good or ill, will not pass. Eternal Love, the reason for being of this world and of all the worlds, this Love shall not be frustrated. *I am the Lord.*

This right of God's is primordial. The right of my parents, my benefactors, my country, my friends, of everyone to whom I recognize some right over my activity, my affection, my devotion, my service — this right is precarious, conditional, limited, subordinate, secondary. I owe them little or much, in truth or perhaps only in my imagination. But I owe *myself* only to God. Only His right is unconditional. He must be served first, for whatever gifts others give me are really His gifts. God first, God served first. *I am the Lord.*

How are we to acknowledge this right?

First of all, we must acknowledge Him with our lips, that is to say, confess Him for what He is, and this leads us to worship, worship without conditions, or restrictions, or limitations: "Tu solus Sanctus, Tu solus Dominus, Tu solus Altissimus."

We must acknowledge Him with our hands, and with our minds that guide our hands, through service: "O Lord, I am thy servant, I am thy servant, the son of thy hand-maid" (Ps. 115:7).

We must acknowledge Him with our hearts, through thanksgiving and love: "Let us therefore love [God], because God first loved us" (1 John 4:19).

The Use of Creatures

God's right extends to all things. And this right is primordial, total, inamissible, eternal, incommunicable. It extends to me. It extends to all the other creatures that necessarily enter my life.

For we are not isolated, autonomous beings, independent of everything and everyone. We are bound to a thousand creatures by bonds of fact or affection, infrangible bonds. Each of us, each human person is the intersecting point and battlefield of innumerable influences, of manifold actions. Humanity is like one of those virgin forests in tropical lands. Each liana, each shoot that climbs up the enormous tree trunks to breathe, to reach the sun and light through the hot and heavy half-night of the undergrowth, is inextricably entangled with the others. It is impossible to touch one of them without making all the others tremble, or pull one out without laboriously disengaging it from the mass of foliage.

How can the right of God be safeguarded in our relations with so many diverse creatures that are constantly influencing us, and to which we are constantly reacting? In this connection St. Ignatius furnishes us precious and very practical light and guidance.

He gives us light when he tells us, after having recalled our fundamental duty, which is to praise, honor, and serve God: "And the rest, all the rest, all that is not God and ourselves, is created for man and to help him to attain his end." These manifold creatures among whom I am thrown, by whom I live, that attract or repel me, some hostile and others friendly, all of them without distinction have a single general goal, as far as I am concerned: they must help me to serve God. That is why they were created.

When, therefore, I seek something else from them, I turn them away from their essential goal. When, for example, I seek in them food to satisfy my sensibilities; an opportunity to develop my personality; an imaginary remedy to my interior troubles by way of reverie; when I seek in them a battlefield for my ambition; a pretext for my melancholy, my sadness, my introspection — in all of these cases and similar ones, I am misusing the providential instrument. And quite naturally, I am punished for it.

If I use a delicate instrument intended to weigh rare substances to weigh a bushel of apples, I break the scales, I make them oscillate wildly. If I try to sew sailcloth with a fine needle, I break the needle and prick myself. Likewise in the spiritual realm, I am the loser each time I make wrong use of a creature, each time I reduce to a selfish, personal use, independent of God, or a fortiori, to a use in opposition to God, a creature that was made to help me to serve Him. This is absolutely self-evident. And the greater the human, carnal success of my usurpation, the greater will be the spiritual deficit. For example, if I make use of my knowledge, my small talents, my faculties, my influence, to make others esteem me for my own sake, to make others love me independently of God, woe to me if I succeed! That makes me refractory, impenetrable to the grace of God.

On the other hand, if I make proper use of these creatures, if I ask of them the thing for which they were made, they will certainly give it to me. They will efficaciously help me to serve God. For then I am using them as God

intended. I am playing on an instrument attuned by God
Himself and His providence. Impossible to sound a false
note.

This is manifestly true of creatures that are at once my
friends and allies in the service of God: my superiors, my
companions, my spiritual exercises, and so on. It is equally
true of creatures that are apparently hostile, unpleasant,
repugnant, afflictive, and even of those that are evil, malicious, impure, enemies of God — such as scandals, demons,
and sinners.

If I ask the former to help me to serve God, they will
lend themselves without resistance, and very often with
great efficacy. This humiliation, this partial setback, this
real or imaginary slight in my regard, this chronic fatigue,
this divergence of views, this spiritual trial, this mourning
that brings grief to those I love, is very often the direct
route over which God's grace will pass. These things are
always an opportunity for me to serve God, if, with God's
grace, I know how to accept them in the right spirit.

And as for the others, creatures in a state of hostility,
of revolt against God, the tempters, the scandalizers, the
occasions of sin, the perverted or subtle attractions; the
still pulsing vestiges of my ancient passions, the live ashes
of the smoldering fires of evil, the disturbing glows that
illumine and point out to my evil desires the house of sin,
the heady suggestions of pride, the paltry bitter delights
of acquiesced sadness — all these creatures, if I ask them
to serve God, will in fact help me to do it. No doubt, at
first they will rebel, they will refuse, they will insult and
mock me. But if I quietly assert myself to them in the
name of God, they will be forced to obey:

"Do not yield to evil, but go forward against it more
boldly."

They will yield with a snarl and under duress, but they
will yield, and they will help us very efficaciously to serve
God.

But how can we obtain this victory? We need practical direction, a method, because many of these creatures are in no sense "tractable"; while the vision is clear, the realization is difficult. There are certain unpleasant, repelling, humiliating creatures that rebuff me to the point that it is difficult for me to turn them to good use, to see in them auxiliaries and messengers of God. Others are so delectable, seductive and charming, that I scarcely know how to close the door upon them when this would be the only way to make them serve the cause of good. How then shall I go about making them help me?

1) By exercising strict control over sensible inclinations and revulsions. This is achieved by obliging them to fast, by reducing them to a secondary role, by strictly measuring out their water and salt, by mortifying them positively, offensively, by attacking them. Example: I have a strong passion for the esteem and affection of others, or perhaps only of certain others. Whence an agitation, a trepidation, that takes away my interior peace every time circumstances recall these persons to my mind, filling me with anxiety about them. "Does he care for me? Is he thinking of me? What can I do for him?" and so on. Whence an obstacle to the spiritual life resulting from this selfish and passionate concern with creatures.

The solution is to deliberately impose a fast upon all that feeds this fire. Let us break off all visits, letters, expressions of affection, pleasurable imaginings, the "application of the senses," in short anything that is not in the nature of a very general and very brief recommendation to God, even an implicit recommendation. And thus we become indifferent. In addition, let us mortify this passion by not reading at once a letter from this person; by avoiding occasions that would remind us of him, by acting as if he were dead for us (for a while) and we likewise dead for him. And so for every other passion: passions of judgment concerning others, of melancholy, of egocentric anxiety.

2) By controlling impassioned attractions and repugnances through retreat and prayer. In retreating, we
refuse them the easy access through which we are almost
always vanquished, we close our door, give ourselves a
little breathing space, and gain time. Prayer too is
necessary.

God is Love

We have seen that God is the Lord, *Ego Dominus,* in
the primary and full sense of the word, and that His right
over us is absolute. We have seen that if we are to acknowledge this right in practice in our lives, we must make use
of creatures in the measure and only in the measure that
they help us to serve God, independently of their power of
attraction or repulsion. This is authentic spirituality and
resolves in principle the practical problems of a truly
faithful life, a life of docility to God.

At the same time, it would be very useful to enlist our
power of loving in this effort. For the work of dominating
creatures, so indispensable for their correct use, is unending, difficult, and sometimes thankless. As the *Imitation of Christ* says: "Love is an excellent thing, a great
good indeed, which alone makes light all that is burden-
some and equally bears all that is unequal. For it carries
a burden without being burdened and makes all that which
is bitter sweet and savory" (Book III, Chapter 5:3).

And it is profitable and easy. For if God is the Lord,
He is also the Father, He is Love: *God is love* (1 John
4:16). Let us concentrate on this one point. Indeed it is
quite obvious that if we fell in love with God's right over
us, with His will which must guide us in the use or depriva-
tion of creatures, we would be powerfully assisted in controlling the natural attractions and repugnances that are
the only obstacle to the enlightened, spiritual, and interior
choice that each of us must make.

God is Love. This signifies first of all that His plans,

His reasons for calling me into life, for creating me and putting me in my place in the order of Providence, are fatherly, benevolent designs, born of His eternal goodness. Regardless of appearances and difficulties, I must remain steadfast in this faith. For everything comes from God, "all is well, all ends with Love" (Blessed Juliana of Norwich).

Into this luminous plan, human and angelic liberty have introduced dark shadows. The fundamental deficiency of every creature makes itself felt. But in the end, God is strongest, God will prevail, God is Love:

"In this faith, I want to live and die!"[1]

God is Love. This also means that the good things, the beautiful things that charm me, that awaken the desire, joy, and enthusiasm that is properly called love — all these things, I say — were made by God. He created them without impoverishing Himself, without diminishing Himself. He has lavished them upon us because it was His good pleasure.

And God possesses within Himself the plenitude of goodness and joy and sweetness. The created things I love are but reflections, echoes, shadows of His perfection. *God is Love.* Everything else is lovable only because it possesses in a partial, ephemeral way what He possesses in its fullness and from all eternity.

Hence let us love Love, let us prefer God, and therefore love and prefer His will. Let us cleave to His will, lose ourselves in it, and care nothing for all the rest, whether attractive or repugnant. Then we shall elect what contributes to the service and glory of Love, of the God who is Love. That is wisdom and justice. It is also an excellent bargain.

"In this faith, I want to live and die!"

God is Love. Finally, this means that we shall find in

---

[1] François Villon, *Ballade pour prier Notre-Dame.*

the love of our God, our Father, our Friend, all the atten-
tions, the marks of tenderness, the gifts, the mutual pleasures and sacrifices that are the bread of the heart, the food
of every authentic love. Yes, we shall find all these things
in Him, but with what purity, what peace, what grandeur!
The initiative is His, and He knows what we are, what we
are worth! "Let us therefore love, because God first loved
us" (1 John 4:19).

Let us turn a deaf ear to the scandalous whisper of our
feeble reason, saying to us: "That is too beautiful to be
true. God cannot love the nothingness that you are! 'Between us and you a great gulf is fixed' (Luke 16:26)." Let
us boldly answer: "God is love. . . . And we have come to
know, and have believed, the love that God has in our behalf" (1 John 4:16). We believe in this love because, in
this great adventure, He reveals Himself to be divine Love,
supreme Love. I believe in this Love:

"In this faith, I want to live and die!"

Suggested Reading

The Gospel according to St. Luke, Chapter 14:25-35; Chapter 13:6-9.

The Imitation of Christ, Book III, Chapters 1 and 2.

INVOCATION TO THE HOLY SPIRIT

Beloved Light, beautiful Light, you banish the night from
our innermost darkness.

Through you the pure are purified, you destroy sin, and
with it the rust it leaves behind.

You make known the truth, you show the path of peace,
and the road of justice.

You flee the hearts of the wicked, you fill the hearts of the
just to overflowing

With the riches of the gift of science.

When you teach, nothing is obscure. When you are present,
nothing is impure. In your presence, the soul is jubi-
lantly secure; conscience rejoices, through you made
joyous, made pure

(Adam of St. Victor † 1192).

I lift up my soul to You, O Lord, like a vessel toward a fountain: fill me [with Your grace] (St. Augustine, *In Psalm.* 142:8).

2.

The Mission of St. John the Baptist

Read: St. Luke 3:1-18, especially verses 3 to 6 on the preparation for the coming of Jesus, and verse 8: "Bring forth therefore fruits befitting repentance." For us, this must consist in making the will of God prevail in our life through virtual prayer, and also in eliminating whatever in us is displeasing to God or less pleasing to Him. And we have the grace to do it.

Sin Outside of Us

We have established ourselves as well as we could in the presence of God and in the fundamental truth: God is the Lord. Fortunately for us, He is also Love. We must therefore serve and honor Him above all else. That is the essential, the Alpha and the Omega of our behavior.

Everything else, notwithstanding any attraction that must be controlled by contemplation and mortification, is made to help us serve God. We must therefore govern the use that we make of creatures according to their aptitudes and their capacities, or on the contrary according to their incapacity to make us serve God.

But there is a real obstacle facing us. It is our attachment to evil, our taste for sin, the disorder of our passions and affections. That is what tends to corrupt our interior life, to darken the light of divine inspiration, and lead us astray in the use we make of creatures.

In his *Exercises,* St. Ignatius makes us look first of all at the obstacle of sin existing outside of us. This is an ingenious idea. For when we look at sin outside ourselves we do not experience the fear and anxiety that make it harder for us to consider sin as it exists within us. We are freer in spirit, calmer. Moreover, since St. Ignatius' purpose is above all to discern and bring to fruition apostolic vocations, the consideration of sin in its effects, its victims, is very important. He broadens out the meditation on sin to the measure of the Kingdom of God, whose only efficacious enemy is sin. It is good for us, therefore, to devote ourselves to this exercise.

The two major examples of sin that St. Ignatius unfurls before us are particularly appropriate: the sin of the angels, and original sin.

1) *The sin of the angels.* This is a sin we find very hard to understand because it is angelic, that is to say, a sin committed by pure spirits living in the fullness of light, supported by great aids, and in no sense tempted by the gross animal motives that are always present in even our most subtle temptations. Theirs was a completely spiritual sin, a sin of complete and willful satisfaction in themselves and in their own excellence, without any reference to God.

The sinning angels said: "I am my own," and not "I am Thine." They refused to give homage to God, their Lord, they refused their love to God, the primordial Love. They denied the right of God. This sin, in view of the plentitude of the angelic knowledge, and in view of the gravity of the abuse thus committed, was a sin against the Holy Spirit. It is the only sin that we can with certitude consider as such, together with the sin of Judas. Hence it was *irremissible.*

What lies between the purity, the nobility, the wealth of affection and adoration, the lucid and peaceful understanding that sees, that exhausts with a single intuition all the accessible intelligibility of a truth or of a being — between this magnificent creature and a demon, a devil, a loathsome tempter, a scurrilous despiser of God, an instigator to every vile action, treason, excess, obscenity, and unclean suggestion? A single sin: a sin of pride.

We can grasp the consequences of this sin, even if its nature is in part beyond our understanding. All that is most completely organized, spiritual, and evil in the greatest crimes is but the pus, pus diluted according to the human mode, of this frightful wound. The most refined blasphemies, the most serious scandals, the most perverse excitations. . . . Let us judge the tree by its fruit, pride by its contagion.

2) *The sin of our first parents* was less grave, since it was remissible and remitted. It was not a sin against the Holy Spirit. It was a sin of human satisfaction, mingled with presumption, curiosity, sensuality, pride, a miserable, grievous human sin, a sin in which all man's instincts and faculties had their part. A very great sin, since Adam and Eve were perfect and enlightened human beings; incomprehensibly greater because they were leaders, the leaders of a whole race, they were a Father and a Mother, heads, persons of responsibility, superiors. . . .

The consequences are visible. As a result of this sin, the whole of posterity, the entire human race came forth wounded, injured, fallen, deprived of its splendid dowry of grace. A sanctuary pillaged, profaned by barbarians, bolsheviks, vandals — what a spectacle! The sacred vessels put to the vilest uses, jeers, sacrilegious parodies, priests tortured and strangled, consecrated virgins scoffed at and martyred. . . .

Such is the picture of our human nature after the storm of original sin. Because of this sin, "all creation groans and travails in pain until now" (Rom. 8:22). Because of it, "I am carnal, sold into the power of sin" (Rom. 7:14). Because of it, our nature is slanted in the wrong direction like a billiard table that slants the balls only one way. Without the constant help of grace, the devil plays his game and wins.

3) Finally St. Ignatius invites us to consider a man who, by reason of a single serious sin, is deprived of grace,

of divine friendship, and becomes a disordered, fallen creature, reproved, damned. He does not tell us that this happens often in fact, nor if it ever happens, nor in what circumstances. He says only this: see the judgment of God on sin that is unquestionably mortal, see its consequences!

A single one of these sins breaks not the bond of fact, for this is infrangible, but the bond of filial love that unites the heavenly Father to His adopted son, the Creator to His creature, He who is to the one who is not. That is a matter of certainty, a truth of faith. A single mortal sin accomplishes what no created power can do — neither the power of Samson nor of Dalila, neither that of Nero nor of the most subtle temptress who ever lived, neither the force of a tempest nor that of a fire, neither the fury of a life that seeks unending pleasure nor of a death that carries all with it, neither the power of men nor of angels. It separates a man from the charity of Christ, it creates an impassable chaos between man and God. The difference between a Paul, a Francis Xavier, a Curé of Ars, a Teresa of Jesus, a Margaret Mary on the one hand and a Judas on the other is only one mortal sin, as far as the essential result is concerned. God's instrument is broken, the vessel of honor is reduced to ignominious, useless, condemned fragments.

Of this we can be sure: "By their fruits you shall know them."

Sin within us

Sin within us: This agent of destruction, of perversion, which we have considered in terms of some of its effects, its radical malice, exists within each of us. We have sinned. We have sinned more or less, according to the graces we have received and to the degree of our fidelity to these graces, but all of us have sinned, and sinned often.

Sins of egoism are particularly easy for us. The majority of our sins that we commit "in succession," sins that do not catch us by surprise but are committed more or less deliberately, stem from deep-rooted selfishness. We have not been willing to forget ourselves, to take the lowest place, to overcome ourselves. We have not been willing to acknowledge at our own expense the sovereign right of God, to prefer the will of God to our own.

Whence those willful states of sadness that are at once the cause and the effect of many sins against resignation, against piety, against charity, against hope. Whence our frequent impatience, our self-satisfaction, our conceited preference of ourselves. Whence our slight sensualities, or our more serious ones, our indulgences, our absence of control, the unleashing of our imagination and sensibilities, our love of pleasure, our passions of all sorts. Whence our countless negligences in the service of God, our refusals of graces, our neglect of inspirations, our rash or hasty judgments. Whence our malicious, indiscreet, or idle words.

All these things are my sinful self, my superficial, evil self. And very often, instead of mortifying it, fighting it, treating it as an adversary, a teacher of error, or as an insignificant factor, I have treated it with consideration, fed it, received it as a friend, as an ally, caressed and cajoled it, accepted it as my master. To this sinful self I have sacrificed my grace-full self, my deeper self, my good self, the son of God and disciple of the Holy Spirit, the friend and servant of Christ, the child of Mary. I have reduced this better self to a minor role, I have reduced it to silence, starved it, ill-treated it, forgotten it, bullied it in a hundred ways. That was evil, because in so doing I have offended God, I have sinned.

Now, each one of my sins has a malice all its own.

1) It is a rich man's sin. Poor women pick up the twigs when the plane trees on the avenue have been pruned, to feed their little fireplaces. In the park of Canterbury alone there is more dead wood than one of these fireplaces could burn in a year. So it is with our vocation. It includes a profusion of graces, enough to enrich twenty, even a hun-

dred wretched human lives. Do you think it is an even
match? No, our refusal of these graces, and especially the
sin that follows from it, is much more serious. And let us
not fall back on the notion that perhaps we are not the
most favored ones. For what do we know about it? We
are still much more favored than the immense majority
of men. The differences among us are differences among
millionaires. We shall be called upon to produce in the
measure of the talents entrusted to us. The man with the
one talent was severely punished for not having earned
another talent.

2) It is an apostle's sin. All these graces have not been
given us for ourselves alone. They are seeds meant to ger-
minate in our field, to fructify, and to give bread to a whole
country: "I have chosen you . . . that you should go and
bear fruit" (John 15:16). If we treat these graces as exclusively our own, if we grind them into flour just to feed
ourselves, if we throw them to the birds on the roadside,
we are unfaithful stewards, we are bankrupting those whom
it is our mission as apostles to help, to lead forward, to save.
We may not know who these persons are, certainly we do
not know them all. But they exist, and "I will require their
blood at your hands, saith the Lord" (cf. Ezech. 3:18).

3) It is a *sin*. That means it is a "No!" said to God,
whether in an important matter or a small one, but a real
"No." It is an offense against the divine Majesty, an infi-
delity against supreme Justice, a refusal to supreme Love.
It is the denial, the scorning of God's right. It is a sin, but
also an error, a foolish act, an incredible blunder. For God
will have the last word, just as He had the first. God does
not lie, He does not forget, He sees the heart: "Man seeth
those things that appear, but the Lord beholdeth the heart"
(1 Kings 16:7).

The Fundamental Virtues — Obedience

We should pass in review a few of these fundamental
and authentic virtues, without which our apostolic life will

be only a phantom, a shadow, a barren field producing only a few scrawny ears of corn lost in a luxuriant vegetation of brambles, nettles, thistles, cockle, poppies, wild oats, cornflowers, plants that may be prickly or lovely but that occupy the earth to no purpose, plants from which no one will ever obtain a handful of flour or a piece of bread.

The first of these virtues, in the opinion of St. Ignatius, is obedience, because "it alone brings forth and sustains the other virtues in our hearts." The spiritual value of obedience comes from the fact that its assiduous and sincere practice is fruitful of every good. In particular, it roots us and makes us grow in humility, patience, and love, which are the three summits of the interior life on earth.

Obedience is the sacrifice of the evil self, the sword that immolates it, a kind of martyrdom, a "good confession" (1 Tim. 6:12). The spiritual value of obedience grows with the moral goodness and all the capacities of the obedient person. The victim is all the more pleasing to God in that it is purer and more beautiful: "If you offer the blind for sacrifice, is it not evil? And if you offer the lame and the sick, is it not evil? Offer it to thy prince, if he will be pleased with it, or if he will regard thy face, saith the Lord of hosts" (Mal. 1:8).

The value of obedience rests in its being truly spiritual, and not carnal, servile, rooted in affection, esteem, or fear that are merely natural and human. For in this latter case there is no longer obedience in the supernatural sense of the word. Authentic, spiritual obedience "sees God in the one who commands on the part of God"; sees "in the superior, whoever he may be, the lieutenant of God and the ordinary, even if fallible, interpreter of His sovereign Will" (St. Ignatius).

Once this is granted, what are the marks of a genuine obedience inspired by the Holy Spirit, apostolic obedience?

1) It is no respecter of persons. That is to say, it sees in the superior, whoever he may be, the interpreter, the

instrument, the lieutenant of God, the representative of God, and therefore obeys equally to the highest superior and "to the subordinate officers who hold their authority from him" (St. Ignatius). It obeys the young as well as the old, the lowliest as well as the most distinguished.

Do we obey in this way? "Be thou ashamed, O Sidon, for the sea speaketh . . ." (Is. 23:4).

2) It is total. That is to say, it abandons to God in the person of the superior, with all the guarantees and precautions that human and Christian wisdom indicate, not merely a few areas of our life, such as our external activities, our professional work. It abandons to Him wholeheartedly and in good faith our interior life as well. How? By impelling us to do well what we are told to do; by making us love and esteem the work that has been entrusted to us. By accepting changes, new starts, fortuitous tasks, substitutions, obligations without any future and devoid of human sweetness. That is heartfelt, filial, spiritual obedience, a "good confession" given after the example of Jesus (cf. 1 Tim. 6:13-14).

3) It is generous and joyous, not constrained and gloomy. That is to say, it is based on authentic faith, on the profound conviction that God who governs by His providence, is Love, and that consequently "all is well, all ends with Love." "To those who love God [and this love is proved first of all by obedience][1] all things work together unto good" (Rom. 8:28). The obedient person is thus assured that his efforts are not lost, that his life serves some purpose, that his field is bearing a harvest, that his apostolic call will not be frustrated.

Whence a profound joy, a joy that tempests, contradictions, interior and exterior sorrows may indeed overcast, and darken for a time, but can never drive away or destroy.

Whence the generosity of the good husbandman, who

---

[1] "He who has my commandments and keeps them, he it is who loves me" (John 14:21).

knows that "he who sows sparingly will also reap sparingly, and he who sows bountifully [with open hands, liberally, opulently, superabundantly] will also reap bountifully" (2 Cor. 9:6). That is why the obedient man is a good rich man, a faithful servant, an efficient apostle.

Is this the way we obey?

Suggested Reading

The Gospel according to St. Luke, Chapter 15.

The Imitation of Christ, Book III, Chapters 50 and 52.

INVOCATION TO THE HOLY SPIRIT

Lifting up the weak,
Guiding the wanderer on his way,
Correcting the erring one,
You sustain the one who wavers,
You help forward the one who strives,
You make perfect the one who loves
(Hildebert of Tours, 11th century).

Spare, O Lord, spare Your people; that having undergone the punishment that they deserve, they may find relief in Your mercy (prayer over the people, Thursday after Ash Wednesday).

Wash yourselves, be clean, take away the evil of your devices from my eyes. Cease to do perversely, learn to do well . . . And then come, and accuse me, saith the Lord. If your sins be as scarlet, they shall be made as white as snow; and if they be red as crimson, they shall be white as wool (Is. 1:16-18).

3.

Fidelity to the Grace of God and Vigilance (according to St. Matthew 25:14-30)

Note Verse 15: "To one he gave five talents [to exploit], to another two, and to another one, to each according to his particular ability. . . ." It is on this that we shall be judged, not by comparisons with others.

Verse 18: The sin of the wicked and lazy servant in this case is not dissipation but negligence to exploit, laziness, scorn, abuse of the graces that invite him to be converted, to do better, to trust. His sin is cowardliness rooted in mistrust.

Verses 24-28: The plea of the negligent one. The Master does not argue with him. He does not accept these undeserved reproaches, but, taking advantage of this answer He overwhelms the negligent one through the very arguments the latter has invoked and that should have made him redouble his vigilance and his fidelity.

Verses 21 and 23: Here the same reward — "I am thy protector, and thy reward exceeding great" (Gen. 15:1) — is given to the faithful servants regardless of the unequal results of their work, because all of them have been "good and faithful" in the few things entrusted to their care.

The Apostolic Profession

Now that we are determined with God's help to purify ourselves — and He will unquestionably give us the grace to do it — let us once again consider the apostolic call we have received from our Lord Jesus Christ.

This call consists first, in aptitudes that the good God has given us to make peaceably the sacrifices indispensable to the apostolic life; second, in attractions that He has given us for the grandeur and usefulness of this life; third, in providential circumstances that have permitted us to hear and to heed the call, to consecrate our life to it. This apostolic call is like a second foundation, a fundamental truth.

It is a fundamental truth in the sense at least that our whole life must, in consequence of this call, take on a new aspect, a special character, a particular orientation. The apostolic vocation acts after the manner of a climate. When you place a living being in a climate warmer or colder than that to which it is accustomed, it must adapt itself in order to live and prosper. Its habitat, its food, its habits, even its tastes will be modified in a new direction. And nothing about this being will be exactly what it would have been in another climate. We who have been called to the apostolate must also take on apostolic ways.

The Exercise of the Kingdom, as St. Ignatius proposes it in his *Spiritual Exercises,* presupposes a man who is unquestionably apt for the apostolate, who has probably been called to it, but who is not yet aware of his call. His concern is to know whether he will follow Christ in the apostolic life, to the point of making the expansion of the Kingdom of God the principal fact of his life, even in the matter of his material occupation. To this end, St. Ignatius encourages, inspires, and spiritually awakens his retreatant, by placing before his eyes by means of a parable the greatness, the beauty, the heroism, and even the usefulness of the apostolic life. Moreover, he probes, tests, and enlightens this man, by frankly explaining to him the real and painful conditions of this life.

As for us who have already chosen, we shall profit greatly by renewing, reawakening, and deepening these views and these sentiments within us, because they will make our vocation at once more dearly loved, more profoundly esteemed, more thoroughly understood, and followed with greater generosity.

The vocation is beautiful and lofty. There is none more beautiful, more useful, or greater. Spiritually speaking, the world can do without illustrious warriors, subtle politicians, and artists of genius. These are the ornaments of the world of spirits, not its constituent elements. As St. Thomas would say, they are "ordered to the perfection of being, not to being pure and simple." We can know God, love and serve Him, live our essential role as reasonable creatures, and save our souls without them. Many are those who get along without them. But in the actual order of Providence, the world cannot do without apostles, because things have been so ordered by God that men must help to save other men. There must be free and responsible intermediaries who are the ordinary impetrators and distributors of God's grace. These men therefore, whatever their apostolic function, are the spiritual leaven of the great human dough, the salt of the earth, and the light of the world.

The exercise of the apostolic profession, so useful in itself, takes on a new beauty and an admirable sweetness from the fact that the apostle, by the very fact that he executes his task to the best of his ability, becomes the collaborator, the companion, and the friend of Jesus Christ. He participates in His divine mission, he makes the infinite graces won by Him bear fruit. In a sense, he is indispensable to Him.

But he likewise shares His way of life: detachment and poverty, at least in spirit; consecration to the work of God; selfless, persevering labor; bearing witness to the Father and to the Holy Spirit. Finally, he shares in His redemption by uniting his sufferings to the Precious Blood of Jesus. In a certain sense, he even shares in His Eucharistic life through the ordinary obscurity of his efforts and their real spiritual efficacy.

Like Jesus, the apostle "has not come to be served but to serve, and to give his life as a ransom for many" (Matt. 20:28). Like Him, he has come to bear witness to the truth: "This is why I was born, and why I have come into the world, to bear witness to the truth" (John 18:37). Like Him, the apostle has "emptied himself" (Phil. 2:7), according to his own measure and in his human fashion. Finally, with Jesus the apostle will share in the final reward: "Father, I will that where I am, they also whom thou hast given me may be with me; in order that they may behold my glory, which thou hast given me" (John 17:24).

The conditions of the apostolic profession are those of Jesus' own life. However, nothing in Jesus stood in the way of the exercise of these difficult virtues, whereas everything in Him was subject and attuned to the most delicate inspirations of the Holy Spirit. The apostle on the other hand owes it to his human condition, to his own weakness and malice, to face up to a preliminary task of spiritual purification and restoration. Doubtless, at this stage of our life, this work has already been accomplished in its essential aspects. But there still remains the task of vanquishing, pursuing, and exterminating interior enemies that are ever raising their heads to threaten and impinge, and that sometimes conquer.

St. Ignatius considers interior enemies whose defeat is the condition *sine qua non* of a serious apostolic life and frankly calls them by their names. First comes sensuality, "contra propriam sensualitatem, si quam habuerint." These words were added to the text as transcribed by Blessed Peter Le Fèvre. This interior enemy is excessive love of sensual or sensible pleasure, the enjoyment of the senses. It involves a delight in ease and comfort, the pleasures of the table, relaxation, the pleasures of the eyes, of human and natural affection, of the imagination, of the sense of touch, from the most gross to the most subtle satisfactions of dilettantism.

In the face of all this, St. Ignatius says that the apostle must "take the offensive." This is not to say that he must deprive himself of everything that is a help, such as a necessary rest, a stimulant to his ministry. But the use of these sensible pleasures must be regulated in the light of apostolic and spiritual exigencies. There must be no concession to sensuality, but a utilization of the sensible within us. And to succeed in this — mortification! This is a word and a reality that we are not too fond of, but that an apostle must never forget: "With Christ I am nailed to the cross" (Gal. 2:19).

The other enemy is carnal and worldly love, that is, attractions and repugnances that are human, carnal, founded on sensibility or vanity, on egoism or self-love, on the desire to enjoy or the desire to shine. These are selfish, self-interested, personal, centripetal attractions and repugnances, and consequently narrow, jealous, exclusive, heavy

with human alloy, depressing, driving us to capitulations
of conscience, to sinful satisfactions, to egoistic sadness,
to intemperate displays, to self-interested lies, to worldly
affections, to rancors born of wounded self-love. In all these
things, take the offensive! The measure of our effort will
be the measure of our apostolic efficacy.

Let us offer ourselves to Jesus to be His apostles at
any cost.

The Offering to the King

St. Ignatius closes the meditation on the Kingdom, on
the apostolic call, by an offering, a prayer, that he calls a
"colloquy," and that is of the greatest significance. This
offering is the prototype of what has become the formula
of the vows in the Society of Jesus. In examining it closely,
we discover it has the same twofold element as does contemplation, of which it is the consummation and quin-
tessence. It contains an element of voluntary offering, of
generosity, of liberality; and also an element of guarantee
and efficacy, so that this offering may be authentic and
produce all its spiritual fruit:

O eternal Lord of all things, I make my oblation to thee,
with thy good pleasure and thy help, in the presence of thy
infinite goodness, under the patronage of thy glorious Mother
and of all the saints of the heavenly court, certifying that I
want, that I desire, that it is my deliberate resolve — provided
it is for thy greater service and thy greater glory — to imitate
thee by enduring all manner of insults and humiliations, and
every form of poverty, both material and spiritual, if thy most
holy Majesty deigns to elevate me to this mode of life and to
receive me into this holy state.

This offering is solemn, voluntary, resolute, and decisive. It is solemn in its tenor which is in the grand style,
made in the presence of God under the patronage of the
Blessed Virgin and of all the saints. It is voluntary: "certifying that I want. . . ." The two wills that are here united,
the divine and the human, are both evoked. As is right,
the initiative as well as the last word are left to the divine
will. Everything is done "with His help," and in accordance

to His good pleasure. But the human will, solicited by the grace of God, has its decisive word to say.

The fact is that, except for rare cases, and regardless of the role played by attraction, by the divine call and inspiration, God deigns to ask from His future apostle — as He once asked His future Mother through the Archangel Gabriel — a free consent. It is a great honor for our human nature, a great delight to our heart. For in the last analysis it depends on us to give to God our Lord something that He deigns to ask of us, a "Yes," a "fiat," an "ecce ancilla Domini," on which all the rest depends.

Finally the offering is resolute and decisive. Indeed, it is formulated in the strongest terms, and with a certain redundancy that is rare for St. Ignatius: "I want . . . I desire . . . it is my deliberate resolution." There is question here of something great, important, serious. It is a matter of following Christ, of saying: "Master, I will follow thee wherever thou goest" (Matt. 8:19). It is a matter of giving ourselves without return, without taking anything back. Our whole life must be and shall be different in consequence of this act.

It is impressive to see how this offering (which is a summing up and completion of contemplation) gives assurance and explicates itself by a sort of guarantee against verbal enthusiasms, against the magic of words, against all that is apparent, superficial, feigned, and false. This is accomplished by the very formula of the offering.

To what end are we offering ourselves? To imitate Christ surely, for without this imitation there is no apostolate. For only that which bears the features of His only-begotten and beloved Son is pleasing to almighty God.

But this general and all-inclusive offering to imitate Jesus is detailed. Here the resolution is so worded as to exclude all dreamers of heroism and parasites of gallantry: "to imitate Thee by enduring all manner of insults and humiliations, and every form of poverty, both material and spiritual."

Only two features of our Master's career, of our Leader's campaign, are retained, no more. Only two episodes are pinpointed: humiliation, poverty. Why? Because fear of them is what keeps many of those who are called from becoming or remaining apostles. Our Lord's love must cloak these terrifying guests so well that, in order to have Him with us, we shall be willing to open the door to them too.

In the mysteries of the cycle of the divine Childhood, that we are asked to contemplate, these essential traits shine forth, and in such simple, lovable, naive forms that we cannot help loving them, or at least enduring them: humiliation in the Mystery of the Incarnation, and poverty in the Mystery of the Nativity.

The Fundamental Virtues — Work

To be equal to his task, the apostle must act against his own sensuality, his natural inclinations, his repugnances born of worldliness and egoism. To this end, nothing will prove more useful than work, if he knows how to make proper use of it. Work is a solid virtue provided only it is practiced apostolically, that is, after the example of Jesus.

In our work, we can roughly distinguish two areas whose frontier varies according to our dispositions, the state of our health, of our nerves. First, the agreeable or at least acceptable type of work. The exercise of a moderate and relatively pleasant, successful activity is always rewarding, and often it is one of the principal delights of life.

For many men — because they are ignorant of prayer or because they make of work a kind of prayer — work is the best part of their day. As an effort is usually made, at least negatively, to put a man at a task that suits his capacities and in which he can succeed, this area of agreeable work is quite extensive.

But there is also an area of laborious, tedious, unpleasant work. For example, the work demanded of us may be too onerous, involve too much overwork. It may give us the impression of always having left something undone. Or perhaps the work required of us is beyond our capacities. Again, it may just be monotonous, tiresome, lacking in human charm.

Apostolic work does not consist in resisting the delight we have in our work which helps us to succeed in it, nor in being immune to the hardships and tedium of certain tasks. Barring extraordinary and special graces, these are inevitable. In what, then, does apostolic work consist?

In the case of *agreeable work,* or work that is at least acceptable, feasible, the apostle must seek the Kingdom of God with singleness of intention, he must seek first to give glory to his Master. His great concern is not his own satisfaction and success but the interests of our Lord Jesus Christ. To this end he must purify his intention. That is the essential point. Everything else will follow from this. The qualities of constancy, steadfast effort, are very easy to acquire in work that we love.

But there is the inevitable danger of taking credit for the fruit of our labors, of taking an owner's satisfaction in them, of glorying in them. For an apostle, that is not permissible. The apostle has given himself, sold himself to God, to work in His vineyard. He is no longer his own, nor is his work his own.

The apostle does not take credit for the fruit of his work. He loves it and delights in it because it is God's field (*agricultura Dei,* as St. Paul says). That is why apostolic work is free of the jealousy, the narrowness of heart that so many owners do not even try to fight. The apostolic laborer is happy to see the Father's harvest grow and ripen, under anyone's hand.

In the case of *tiresome, difficult work,* whatever the cause and the degree, the apostle finds an occasion for considerable apostolic merit and reparation within his reach, an opportunity for very pure love. It is an opportunity for merit, because it is the unquestioned fulfillment of the will of God. When the apostle approaches this type of work, he can say: "Not as I will, but as Thou willest." He accepts it gladly, although he would never have chosen it himself.

It is also an opportunity for reparation, because it is a penance. And it is a penance that is not merely permitted, but actually counseled, imposed upon him, and in which self-love, self-satisfaction, and free choice have no part.

It is an opportunity for very pure love because this thankless work is commanded by love and rewarded by it. It is impossible to do it well, generously, humbly, without receiving a reward from God for our effort in the form of an increase in His love.

The only condition for our reaping these great spiritual benefits is that we work in a filial spirit, and not like hired laborers who are hurrying to complete at all costs work that holds no interest for them. Work, and especially hard, unpleasant work, is just as much the *opus Dei* for the apostolic worker as is the chanting of the Office for the Benedictine monk. It is a kind of contemplation, laborious contemplation, a form of *purification through action*.

Suggested Reading

The Epistle to the Philippians, Chapter 1, and Chapter 2, verses 1 to 18.

The Imitation of Christ, Book II, Chapters 7 and 8.

INVOCATION TO THE HOLY SPIRIT
At once Gift and Giver,
You are our hearts' whole treasure,
Make our hearts apt for Your praise,
Form on our lips words to celebrate Your glory.
Purify us of our sins,
Author of all purity,
And to Your faithful renewed in Christ,
Give in plenitude the joys of perfect newness
(Adam of Saint Victor).

For I will . . . bring you into your own land. And I will pour on you clean water, and you shall be cleansed from all your filthiness, and I will cleanse you from all your idols. And

I will give you a new heart, and put a new spirit within you; and I will take away the stony heart out of your flesh, and will give you a heart of flesh. And I will put my spirit in the midst of you, and I will cause you to walk in my commandments (Ezech. 36:24-27).

If any man does not love the Lord Jesus Christ, let him be anathema (1 Cor. 16:22).

4.

The Two Standards

Once St. Ignatius has clearly formulated the apostolic call and its real conditions, he pursues his task of apostolic formation with a twofold series of exercises. First, the contemplation of the mysteries of the divine Childhood brings out vividly the essential virtues that are the conditions for an efficacious apostolate: the humiliation of the Incarnation; the poverty of the Nativity; the affective detachment of the Presentation; the effective detachment in the episode of the twelve-year-old Christ in the Temple, etc.

Then come exercises in which each individual faculty is given the opportunity to face up to what seems hardest for it, and consequently exercises, inures itself, purifies itself of its dross, and overcomes its disorders. In the "Two Standards," the faculty of the intellect is in question; in the "Three Classes of Men," it is the will; and in the "Three Degrees of Humility," the faculty in question is that of the affections. At the end of this formation, carried on simultaneously in part, with all possible sincerity and intensity, a man is in the best disposition to make the right election, uninfluenced by human motives and passions.

We should note in passing that St. Ignatius is too good a psychologist to compartmentalize the human faculties in this way, since they always function together and influence one another. What he does is give each in turn the nourishment best suited to it.

The exercise of the intelligence is destined to make the retreatant understand better the tactics of the two generals who are fighting over his activity.

The essence of the parable of the "Two Standards" is as old as Christianity itself, that is, in a sense as old as the world. It is the "life and death in a wondrous conflict joined"; it is the Two Cities of St. Augustine. St. Ignatius takes up this theme again in a military guise, perhaps because of the Gospel parable of the "strong man armed" (cf. Luke 11:21-23). More probably he does so because being a soldier in his very soul he sees things from the military point of view. But we could very easily transpose it, for example, into the "Two Dwellings" or the "Two Palaces," imagining the one to be the home of the Devil, the prince of those powers of darkness against whom St. Paul sets us on our guard, and the other Christ's humble dwelling, His modest palace. In the former all is ostentation, excitation, sham, make-believe, imitation, temptation, sensuality, lewdness. In the latter, all is sincere, simple, true, authentic, pure and beautiful, innocent and peaceful.

Indeed the lesson is the same. When the man in question is one who has overcome or at least unmasked and fled the temptations of the flesh, so that he must be tempted under the colors of goodness, the devil uses a trap with three compartments arranged successively in depth, like hoopnets or weirs for catching fish. They are drawn tighter and tighter, in such a way that if one is able with difficulty to escape the second, there is no escape from the third where the bait has been placed.

The first compartment of the trap is the spirit of spiritual or temporal wealth, the spirit of ownership that makes us treat persons and things (certain persons and certain things) as belonging to us, as our very own, and having no right to refuse to give us themselves or anything else. Whence a sentimental attachment that sometimes goes as far as passion. Whence a tendency to trust the temporal, the carnal.

The tempter makes his dupe pass from this attachment, from this love of riches into the compartment of vain honor, of vanity, of demanding, pretentious, easily ruffled conceit. We are pleased with ourselves, we think we are inadequately understood, helped, esteemed, honored, thanked, set apart.

From this it is but a step to the "great pride," to use the expression of St. Ignatius. And then the fish is caught, caught insofar as it can be here on earth, for there is always the possibility of escape even from pride, but it is easier to escape gross carnal pride than the subtle spiritual pride born of ambition.

The tactics of the good Master, of the legitimate Master, our Lord, are diametrically opposed. They stem from the First Beatitude and lead in three stages, in three ascents, to the mountain of Humility, from which all spiritual good and all apostolic fruitfulness flow, because God exalts the humble.

The first stage is affective disappropriation, the spirit of poverty, of self-stripping, of detachment, dedication, spiritual liberty. This spirit is compatible with great material riches. It is easily compatible with the use of modest goods in a simple life like ours. It is incompatible only with attachment to riches, whatever their nature. This spirit consists in substituting the right of use for the right of ownership, just as one uses various articles in a hotel or a hospital. This spirit applies to the spiritual riches of affection as well. *Laqueus contritus est* — the snare is broken. The apostle is free.

From these first steps the candidate-apostle is led by Jesus to a higher, steeper hill, characterized by a transparent atmosphere of simplicity and sincerity, an absence of pretension to the point of complete self-forgetfulness; a facility for living to the point of total interior renouncement. To be reprimanded, to be put in one's place — there to be silent or to speak only when necessary — these things are hard for some people. To accept our defeats, our fate, our task, our weaknesses, our involuntary faults: this is the second liberation of which the *Imitation of Christ* speaks.

From this height we reach the summit of the mountain of Humility. And here, "haurietis aquas in gaudio de fontibus Salvatoris — you shall draw waters with joy out of the Savior's fountains" (Is. 12:3). The apostle has been formed. "This man is a chosen vessel to me" (Acts 9:15).

Jesus in the Temple

After exercising our intellects to purify ourselves of self-interested views distorted by selfish passions (the Exercise of the "Two Standards"), we must now exercise our will. To this end, we might meditate upon the Exercise of the "Three Classes of Men." But it will be more pleasant and perhaps even more profitable to take as the object of our contemplation our Lord and His Mother in one of their mysteries best suited to strengthen our apostolic resolutions.

It is the mystery that shows us the boy Jesus at the age of twelve, remaining in the Temple unbeknown to His Mother and His adopted father. Saint Luke records the fact in Chapter 2, verses 41 to 52. This is an important and deeply mysterious episode. And yet a few essential points and primordial lessons clearly emerge from it.

It was the first apostolic initiative of Jesus' career. He was twelve years old, the "coming of age" for Israelite adolescents, if we dare say so. Until that time, the son, even the oldest son, was an inseparable part of the family. From then on, he was an autonomous member of the faithful, personally subject to the obligations of the law. On this occasion, Jesus wanted to stress the fact that His life belonged to the Kingdom of God, to the interests of His heavenly Father; that He had come to be an apostle, to serve, to bear witness to the Truth and to give His life for the redemption of many.

The mysterious thing is that this act, intended to affirm His mission, to reveal His vocation, to be a milestone, was accomplished without any preliminary notice to Mary and Joseph and under circumstances that on the contrary were calculated to grieve them deeply. And they were indeed grieved: "Behold, in sorrow thy father and I have been seeking thee" (Luke 2:48).

Jesus answered this very natural and restrained complaint by making a declaration of principle, an assertion of His independence as an apostle, which must have seemed very cruel to those to whom it was addressed: "Did you not know that I must be about my Father's business?"

Manifestly, here is a lesson in absolute apostolic detachment. It is not contrary to the Fourth Commandment of God. It does not deny or condemn any of the holy and divinely instituted affections of the family. But it affirms, in the particular case of the apostolic vocation, that this familial affection, this natural love must be ready for complete immolation, ready to immolate in the apostle's heart the joys of sensible presence; ready to demand of the apostle's parents, with all possible circumspection, the immolation of the joys of sensible presence. The apostle and his parents have the grace for it. In exchange for this great sacrifice, they will receive rewards of a spiritual nature and eternal value out of all proportion to the sacrifice itself. That is certain.

As to the extent of this sacrifice, in general it should be reduced for others in the measure that it is necessary, and it must be accepted for oneself in the full measure of God's call. Obedience is the only reliable and pacifying rule, at least in the beginning and for a certain time. Faith and trust are nowhere more necessary than on this point, as is recourse to the Blessed Virgin Mary.

Faith is the more necessary inasmuch as this sacrifice is very often not understood. Even Joseph and Mary, despite the admirable elevation and purity of their views, "did not understand" at the time what Jesus said to them. All the more reason why (even though the circumstances are entirely different and infinitely less mysterious) we cannot expect prompt or perfect understanding of this matter by our loved ones. More often than not, their attitude will be one of passive, painful resignation, and it will ordinarily take a long time for this resignation to become peaceful, illumined by supernatural faith. Sometimes acceptance will be accompanied by bitter reproaches or piercing laments: "Son, why hast thou done so to us?" The only thing we can do in such instances is to hold fast, to be silent, to pray, to give a few good reasons that will not appear so until much later. It is a cross, sometimes a real martyrdom, but it is the door to the apostolate.

The apostle, by definition, is the man who tears others away from the temporal, the carnal, the human, in order to make them cleave to the spiritual, the eternal, the supernatural. His voice will be convincing, penetrating, only if he himself has made the necessary sacrifices, if he has detached himself with faith and love from the things of earth. In the words of St. Ignatius, he must have torn himself away from "the affection that flesh and blood are accustomed to give to parents and close relatives." This total affective detachment, effective in the measure of each individual destiny, is the condition *sine qua non* of the apostolic life. And this is the second lesson of this mystery.

"And His Mother kept all these things carefully in her heart" (Luke 2:51). It is she no doubt who has handed this account down to us. We shall ask her heart to enable us to understand it. It is touching to see Mary thus treated by God and by her own Son, "like a little girl" if we dare say so. No reasons are given her. There is no fear of testing her or astonishing her. She is treated as an *instrument* of the Kingdom of God, and this disposition of Providence is both profound and admirable. But if God acts in this way with regard to the innocent, immaculate, most enlightened and privileged Mother of God, should I complain if God asks me to walk in obedience, in the darkness of pure faith, and in filial abandonment?

The Fundamental Virtues — Self-Forgetfulness

In the Exercise on the "Two Standards," we have already spoken of the self-forgetfulness which leads to humility the man who has conceived the spirit of poverty. This virtuous disposition of self-forgetfulness is so important that it is good to pause a little and consider it.

It is particularly indispensable to the exercise of fraternal charity. Without self-forgetfulness we are in danger of not giving ourselves to our brothers, of being lone wolves, of remaining isolated in our egoism, our sadness, our petty personal passions. Or of creating a schism in the community, of creating a narrow, closed, exclusive group of two, three, or four persons, that saps the milk of charity the way a sucker draws off the sap from the main stem of a rose bush.

Let us explain ourselves very simply on this point.

The first case is that of a person so engrossed with himself, with his search for his own selfish pleasure, that he is walled up, isolated, and constantly focussing his attention on his own life. A person with such a character evaluates everything, including the vicissitudes of his spiritual life, in relation to the development, the enjoyment, the possession of his "ego." He is very often absorbed by his real or imaginary sufferings, by the insufficiencies, the lacks, the melancholy that assail every human life. Depending on his temperament, he becomes hard or breaks. He falls back into a sort of haughty insensibility or melts into a whining self-pity. He becomes a man of marble or of wax, quick to sneer or to weep. But always, such a person isolates himself.

Well now, child of God, chosen soul, candidate for the apostolate, servant of the Great King, friend of Jesus Christ, *what about the others?* What about the welfare, the tranquility, the peace, the joy, and the consolation of the others? What about your family, your friends, your fellow workers? Where are your desires, your promises, your apostolic efforts? Where is your Master and your God: "Ubi est Deus tuus?"

Truthfully, you are acting like an egoist, nursing your

sorrow, your troubles, your imaginings. You are neither wise, nor faithful, nor docile to God. You are turning your back on the apostolate. Instead of helping and loving and rejoicing others, you are a constraint, a dead weight, a permanent sadness. Instead of filling the landscape with sunshine, you cover it with fog, you make it ugly. Instead of making the atmosphere brighter and lighter, you weigh it down and make it unbreathable.

For some, pursuit of self and of their own pleasure does not take on this exclusively personal form. Instead, their concern is focussed on a narrow, absorbing group which may consist of only one person or of a few favorites. Whence comes a schism, a self-contained clique, if these persons fall in with the game and return familiarity for familiarity. Whence a lasting sadness and loneliness if these persons, wiser and more faithful to God, refuse to share these private affections, or do so only with a cautious and supernatural spirit. In this latter case, our egoist falls back into the attitude and the sentimental anxieties of the isolated person. The detriment to the community is less than in the former case, but his desolation and distress are all the more poignant.

If on the other hand we make self-forgetfulness the basis of the life of charity, the result is joy, common good feeling, tender charity, a limpid and shining atmosphere like that of a beautiful summer evening. In short, it is one of the principal strengths and joys of an apostle's life. Why?

Because when we forget ourselves, the qualities, virtues, talents, and aptitudes needed to fashion and enrich life in common can develop and grow. A true family life can unfold, free of defects and exclusivism. Self-forgetfulness suppresses almost automatically, if we dare say so, the dangers of vanity and self-seeking. The barriers erected between individuals by timidity, divergences in tastes, education, and aptitudes, are overcome or at least greatly reduced, leaving only what is needed to assure the variety, richness, and piquancy of life in common. When these purified and liberated forces are given free play, the joys of the common life reach their height. Then all live for each one, and each one lives for the others.

Self-forgetfulness likewise liberates the supernatural and apostolic spirit, enabling it to make rapid progress. For once egoism is vanquished, unity of intention and spirit reign. And all the fruits of the Holy Spirit — "charity, joy, peace, patience, kindness, goodness, faith, modesty, continency" (cf. Gal. 5:22) — ripen and scent the air.

Suggested Reading

The Imitation of Christ, Book III, Chapters 15 and 23.

The Gospel according to St. Luke, Chapter 2.

INVOCATION TO THE HOLY SPIRIT

O Fire, Spirit Paraclete,
Life of the life of every creature,
You are holy, giving life to forms!
You are holy, healing dangerous fractures!
You are holy, binding fetid wounds!

(Saint Hildegarde).

The Lord wants gentle mounts; be the Lord's mount, that is to say, be gentle.

It is He who sits upon you, it is He who guides you. Have no fear of stumbling or falling into the precipice.

The horse and the mule sometimes raise their heads and rear so furiously that they throw over their rider. They are tamed by means of the bridle, the bit, blows, until they learn to submit and to bear their master. As for you, do not wait until the bridle bruises your mouth. Be meek and bear your Lord (St. Augustine, *in Psalm.* 33, 5).

5.

The Spirit of Jesus

The human, natural, carnal spirit — even the most excusable and in a sense respectable such as that of St. Salome — is always imbued with a certain egoism, a certain narrowness, a rather childish and often futile ambition.

Let us picture the scene so vividly described by St.
Matthew: St. Salome entreating favors for her sons at the
Master's feet. In answer to Our Lord's question: "What
dost thou want?" she immediately expressed her demand
with all her mother's passion (cf. Matt. 20:21). But His
answer was not the one she expected. It was a serious
reprimand followed by a very clear summons. The two
brothers, "sons of thunder," somewhat abashed but still
brave and resolute in their love of Jesus, answered without
a moment's hesitation: "We can [drink of this cup]."
Jesus then briefly assured them that their pledge would
have its effect, and avoided the mother's initial request.

The indignation of the ten other disciples (Matt. 20:24)
is very instructive. It is permissible to think that they
too would have made or at least let someone else make on
their behalf the request Salome made for her sons. But
since only the two brothers had in fact been compromised,
they became the object of general indignation.

Jesus took advantage of this situation to define the
essential contents of the "cup" that His true disciples must
be ready to drink: effective obedience, service, sacrifice,
including the sacrifice of their lives (cf. Matt. 20:25-28).
Here is a compelling summary of the apostolic call and of
the authentic spirit of Jesus.

Are we ready to say "We can!"? We must understand
to what we are pledging ourselves. But it is the cup of
Jesus, "my cup."

Conforming to the Tastes of Christ

At this point in St. Ignatius' *Exercises,* the retreatant is
made to look his life straight in the face, and to make a
choice. It is the election of a state of life, the culminating
point of the *Exercises.* And he is now ready to make this
choice, for he has been enlightened by the light of fundamental truth and the light of the divine call of Jesus the

King. The exercises on sin have purified him, meditation on the mysteries of the divine Childhood and on the "Two Standards" has liberated him from the disordered passions that might still darken his judgment and complicate his intentions, preventing him from being docile to God.

For us, the choice has already been made, and barring some rare exception there is no reason to go over it again except to confirm it, to renew our dedication to the apostolic life which by the grace of God we have chosen and to which many of us are already vowed. This reform, this confirmation involves two stages: the first is the reasoned and divinely inspired choice of certain resolutions, certain improvements in our life; the second is the development within us of the tastes of Christ the Redeemer.

As a rule, the resolutions become progressively simpler and more general. The choice must be determined by the obstacles to God's grace that still remain within us; and also by the attraction that our Lord gives us, that the Holy Spirit places in our hearts for the virtues opposed to our faults, to our disordered passions, to our vicious and sinful tendencies.

Often, very often, it will be easy to discover abuses to be corrected, especially if we have exterior faults that are visible, serious, reprimanded by our conscience. For example, we may be gloomy, ill-tempered, easily upset in certain circumstances. And if our interior faults are at all serious, we cannot help being aware of them through our examinations of conscience for Confession. Our imagination may be exuberant, all-absorbing, leaving little or no room for converse with God, no time for prayer. Or perhaps we love one or another person (and this person may be ourselves) too passionately, too naturally. Whence come excessive anxieties, melancholy, jealousies. Again, we may be spiritually lazy, neglecting or rushing through the most essential exercises of our religious life. We may make no regular effort to serve and love God, dropping everything

if the inspiration of the moment is lacking. We may
tolerate vast deserts in our life, in which we allow ourselves
to live the good life of nature without thinking of God any
more than if He did not exist, or were not calling us to His
service.

In all of these cases we need to make a few short
practical resolutions. Such resolutions must always be
founded on abnegation, self-forgetfulness, trust, and the
spirit of faith. They always lead us in the direction intended by the Holy Spirit when we are docile to Him, when
we are well disposed and happy to be in God's service.

It may be that we can find no serious, visible fault calling for prompt and firm reform. Perhaps our failings are
more like a dust-cloud of vain trifles, imperceptible weaknesses, small laxities. Or again the obstacle to grace within us may be so deeply a part of our temperament and
habits as to be almost immune to direct attack. It may be
a constitutional disorder, so to speak, rather than a visible
and palpable defect. In that event, we must respond to the
attractions that the good God gives us when we are peaceful and happy in His service, eager for goodness, and faithful to the Holy Spirit.

We must nurture this divine attraction within us and
defend it against the subtle recurrences of sentimental
complications, self-love, self-will, and self-concern. Then
we shall be drawn toward self-forgetfulness, abandonment,
trust, intimate union with Jesus, and the faithful imitation
of Mary's virtues.

In every case we must conform with our whole will,
with our whole heart to the tastes of Christ the Redeemer.
That is St. Paul's advice: "Have this mind in you which
was also in Christ Jesus" (Phil. 2:5). The tastes of Jesus
must become a part of us. To this end, St. Ignatius proposes to us as our principal objects of contemplation the
mysteries of the suffering and glorious Jesus. That is the

cycle of the third and fourth weeks of the *Exercises,* which we must here reduce to a few examples.

The third week is intended to make the retreatant love the tastes of Christ the Redeemer as they were manifested during His sorrowful Passion. Here is an immense and infinitely touching reservoir that each Christian generation has meditated upon without ever exhausting it. Each generation has sought in it the remedy, the consolation, the stimulant it needed most, that corresponded best to its needs and attractions.

The preferences of our own time, which we and those among whom we must exercise our apostolate necessarily share, are tendencies to pride, autonomy, and excessive independence. These tendencies are apparent even in our vanity, our unconventional attitudes, the immodesty of our dress, our freedom of opinion, our manners, our reading, conversation, entertainments and pleasures. In all these things, it is not so much pleasure we seek (and here I am talking of women) as independence, emancipation, a sort or revenge for the subjection of former times. It is against this form of pride and curiosity that we must fight hardest, both within us and outside of us.

The Passion offers us a hundred admirable examples to help us. Here the tastes of Christ are revealed with incomparable clarity, and notably His taste for dependence, submission, self-abnegation. In this connection St. Paul reminds us of the point of departure of the Word Incarnate, namely, essential, inalienable glory: "who . . . was by nature God . . . [and] equal to God" (Phil. 2:6). And likewise St. John: "knowing that the Father had given all things into his hands, and that he had come forth from God and was going to God . . . (John 13:3). "You call me Master and Lord, and you say well, for so I am" (John 13:13).

Keeping this in mind, we see the attitude that expresses the taste of Christ, His preference, His free choice, His voluntary election: "[He] emptied himself, taking the

nature of a slave . . ." (Phil. 2:7); "[He] rose from the
supper and laid aside his garments, and . . . he poured water
into the basin and began to wash the feet of the disciples"
(John 13:4-5).

The great abasement, the great abnegation, the great
annihilation, the great dependence, the great service is first
of all the Incarnation. Everything else flows from that.
But the Passion of Christ presents this voluntary annihilation, this painful, humiliating, dependent service in its
paroxysm, at its point of supreme intensity: "wounded, as
one struck by God, despised, and the most abject of men,
a man of sorrows" (cf. Is. 53:2-8). It represents everything that abases, breaks, diminishes, kills, annihilates a
man: chains, outrages, abandonments, denials, derisory or
degrading condemnations, ridicule, blows, death. . . .

This in all truth is the first voluntary taste of Jesus.
And He offered Himself up freely: "He was offered because
it was his own will" (Is. 53:7). For such was His good
pleasure. "The Son of Man has not come to be served but
to serve, and to give his life as a ransom for many" (Matt.
20:28). That is why He came. If anyone wants to follow
Him, therefore, to share in His work, to be the companion
of His labors, His life, and of His glory, he must abase himself, he must serve, he must obey, he must subordinate
himself, and enter the ranks.

If anyone wants to follow Christ he must serve in his
vocation, that is, he must abase himself willingly and resolutely, accept obscure tasks, drudgery, life in common.
He must accept as his due, as good, desirable, venerable, the
portion of abasement and humiliation that life, that the
providence of God has in store for him: failures, stalemates,
painful subjections, helplessness, chronic illness, unreward-
ing work, unjustified criticisms, and justified reproaches
that are even more cruel. In short, *he must serve.*

The Obedience of Jesus

We meditated above on the primary taste of Christ: "He emptied Himself," He abased and humbled Himself, He obeyed. In the same passage urging us to conform ourselves to the sentiments, tastes, and preferences of Christ, St. Paul completes his brief portrait of the Word Incarnate with these words: "becoming obedient to death, even to death on a cross" (Phil. 2:8).

This taste of Jesus is the consequence and complement of the first, which it incarnates in the supreme act of the Crucifixion, the peak of the spiritual summit that is the Passion of Christ. This is obedience, submission to God His Father, painful obedience, blind and absolute submission even to the most ignominious, the most notorious, the most cruelly exemplary of deaths, death on a cross. Jesus loves obedience so much that He has assumed a human nature in order to be capable of this submission, of this virtue.

This obedience blazes forth during the Passion. It is then that it presses down on Jesus with its full weight, on Him who said: "My food is to do the will of him who sent me" (John 4:34), of Him who found such delight in cleaving to the will of His Father: "I praise thee, Father . . . for such was thy good pleasure" (Luke 10:21; cf. parallel passages), and who now said: "Father, if thou art willing, remove this cup from me; yet not my will but thine be done" (Luke 22:42).

Our Lord pushes away this cup of bitterness and shame, overflowing with every manner of impurity, with the filthy potions of all sinners. It nauseates Him to the point of terror, of causing a bloody sweat, of throwing Him into an agony (cf. Luke 22:43).

And finally on the Cross, He feels the terrible sanctity of Justice hurtling down upon His heart, and He cries out, attributing to Himself the plaints of the just man, suffering

and apparently abandoned: "My God, my God, why hast
thou forsaken me?" (Matt. 27:46). But in the end, His
love for the will of the Father assumes control, dispels the
storm, and shines like a brilliant sun over the desolate land:
"Shall I not drink the cup that the Father has given me?"
(John 18:11). "Father, into thy hands I commend my
spirit" (Luke 23:46).

We want to obey with Jesus, like Jesus, for Jesus. Not
with a passive, automatic, brutal submission, with the subjection of a gross, stupid serf, with a heart of stone; not
with the servile obedience of a beaten dog, of a lackey who
takes his revenge for his forced submission by means of
irony, sneering, and the spreading of gossip. No, ours must
be the free obedience of sons, living, smiling, and supernatural; an obedience full of initiative and love, the obedience of the heart of flesh.

This obedience is founded first of all on the recognition
of the identity, as a general rule, between the will of the
Father and the commands, instructions, and counsels of
His authorized interpreters. "He who hears you, hears me;
and he who rejects you, rejects me" (Luke 10:16). It is
also founded on the voluntary sacrifice of what is dearest,
most intimate to us: our own judgment, our autonomy, our
freedom. When thus understood and practiced, this obedience is our choice, crucifying us to the world and the world
to us. "With Christ I am nailed to the cross" (Gal. 2:19).
"But as for me, God forbid that I should glory save in the
cross of our Lord Jesus Christ, through whom the world
is crucified to me, and I to the world" (Gal. 6:14).

We want to obey with Mary, like Mary, who accepted
the will of God throughout her life, but notably on the day
of the Presentation, on the day she found Jesus in the
Temple, on the day of the Passion. At every moment she
accepted the severe, the august, the terrifying, mysterious,
and adorable will of God. She accepted it totally, to the end,
to the death of her Son, and to His death on the Cross.

The Fundamental Virtues — Interior Mortification

St. Paul says everything there is to say on this subject: "For you have died and your life is hidden with Christ in God" (Col. 3:3). This means: "You have died to evil, to sin, to the carnal, and your new, spiritual, holy life is hidden with Christ, with His example, His grace, His love, in God."

This death to evil, to the interior enemy, to the obstacle to the reign of God within us is called interior mortification or purification. Exterior penance is but the fruit of this interior activity, or the means of obtaining it, depending on whether it is expiation for our own sins, or reparation for those of others.

This interior purification or mortification consists of a series of detachments, strippings, partial deaths, that touch us progressively more deeply and more painfully. But Our Lord's call to us and His grace make them constantly easier and often very sweet. Let us pass in review in an ascending order a few of these strippings, a few of these partial deaths to evil.

We must die to sensuality by purifying, by mortifying our sensible self. For example, we must overcome our gluttony either by depriving ourselves of pleasant foods or by their moderate use, or perhaps by forcing ourselves to eat enough, regularly and slowly. We must overcome curiosity by the modesty of the eyes, by a certain reserve in our manifestations of affection, even the most innocent, and by silence. We must overcome our love of pleasure by a life that is somewhat rugged, stern, controlling unnecessary fatigue, fighting neurosis and its causes, that is to say excessive, unreasonable, depressing reactions to our ills or troubles, whether real or imaginary.

We must die to our own point of view, by mortifying, by purifying our own ideas. Attachment to their own views is the pride of spiritual men and often makes their souls impermeable to grace, gives them hearts of stone. This is very important, for we often accept everything, including

effort and hardship, on condition that our own ideas prevail. We rarely accept any but our own views, we are
obstinate and diabolically clever in camouflaging our own
point of view with good reasons. We often condemn, criti-
cize, argue with, or judge authority; we begrudge it because it has decided differently than we. Then we work
with bad grace, and we rarely accept reprimands when they
bear on our cherished opinions or ideas.

This attachment to our own ideas is harmful to humility,
charity, and obedience. It lessens the efficacy of our prayers, and reduces our efforts to a purely human level lacking
in spiritual fruitfulness. We must overcome this tendency
by exterior and interior silence in the presence of whatever
displeases, wounds, grieves, or surprises us about the
decisions of authority. Also by being patient and meek
when others refuse to give us, or defer granting what we
ask; when others tell us to change our ways of doing and
acting. We must also pray to this end, and strive to enter
into the views of others, especially of our superiors, but
also of our equals and inferiors when these views differ from
our own.

We must die to idleness, to ambition, as well as to spiritual timidity, laziness, and cowardice. In our interior life,
there is ample matter for mortification, for meritorious and
necessary purification. Hence, we must die to our overly
natural desire to see, control and judge everything in our
spiritual life; to know exactly where we stand and at what
degree of perfection; to progress only on terrain we know
and recognize in advance. We must die to our fear of
risks, of the unknown, of losing our footing. We must die
to our tendency to give only partial, carefully guarded and
controlled trust to our spiritual guides.

We must die to the human and natural fear of serving
God too well, of yielding without condition to His inspirations, to the direction of our superiors; to the fear of being
too unhappy, of being forced to go beyond what we want
to or can sacrifice, if we do what they say. We must die

to the desire for spiritual delights, for the favor of pleasurable mental prayer. We must die to our preference for these pleasures over the solid virtues of obedience, abnegation, humility, and self-forgetfulness. And likewise we must die to the fear that spiritual aridity, trials, temptations, distractions, darkness, and other spiritual troubles may surpass our strength, may last all our lives, may be too much for the grace we have received.

Although such purification may seem formidable from a distance, it is most desirable because it is accomplished *with Christ in God.*

The Compassion of the Blessed Virgin Mary

Meditation on the fact of the Compassion, notwithstanding the power of Mary's faith. (Cf. the beautiful Lessons of the Second Nocturn of the Office of Our Lady of Sorrows by St. Bernard.)

Once this has been done, we shall contemplate the Compassion of Mary during the hours when uncertainty as to her Son's exact fate aggravates her suffering, as she sees Him ill-treated, unjustly judged and condemned. May our own incertitude and anxiety, our anguish for those we love be sanctified by union with the Compassion of Mary.

The Compassion of Mary when Jesus, having been condemned and laden with His Cross, goes up to Calvary. This time, it is the end. He will die. In a few hours, all will be consummated. Let us unite our bereavements beyond human remedy.

The Compassion of Mary during the hours Jesus is agonizing on the Cross in extreme pain, extreme shame, extreme abandonment — even, in terms of human feeling, abandonment by His Father.

Three nails pierce the Mother's heart as they fasten the innocent body of her Son to the Cross. Let us unite our sufferings, shames, and humiliations, our spiritual trials, to hers. The sum total of our sufferings is so infinitesimal by comparison with Mary's, but each one of us can still say: this is my cross!

The Compassion of Mary when the lifeless body of her Son is laid in her arms. Let us look and feel:

> Virgin of all virgins blest . . .
> Let me, to my latest breath,
> In my body bear the death
> Of that dying Son of thine.

Suggested Reading

The Gospel according to Saint John, Chapters 18 and 19.

The Imitation of Christ, Book III, Chapters 27, 32, and 37.

INVOCATION TO THE HOLY SPIRIT

O Voice that speaks without noise of words,
O penetrating Voice, secret Voice,
Voice whispered into your blessed disciples' ears!
O sweet Voice, O beloved Voice,
Resound in our minds.
Light that dispels error,
Light that brings the truth within us,
Confer upon us life and health and eternal glory

(Adam of Saint Victor).

How I hunger, how I thirst for you during my pilgrimage here below, Lord, so that your presence may some day fill me to satiety!

The world draws me by so many beautiful, powerful, diverse things: you are more beautiful, you who made them; more powerful and more glorious, you who made them; sweeter, you who made them! (Saint Augustine, *Sermo* 158, 7).

God asks of you not words but your heart (Saint Augustine, *in Psalm.* 134, 11).

He was offered because it was his own will (Is. 53:7).